Laurence-Khantipalo Mills was ordained as a novice in 1959, in England. A year later, he was ordained as a monk (bhikkhu) in India. After three years in India, he travelled tô Thailand, where he was reordained in 1966, with Venerable Somdet Phra Nyanasamvara, the abbot of Wat Bovoranives Vihara, Bangkok, as his preceptor. For the next eleven years he lived and studied in Thailand, practicing meditation with various teachers in the forests of northeast Thailand and writing several books published by Mahamakut Press in Bangkok and the Buddhist Publication Society in Sri Lanka.

In 1973, he was invited by his preceptor to help establish a Thai Buddhist temple in Sydney, Australia, now known as Wat Buddha-rangsee in Stanmore. He taught meditation at several locations, and in 1978 became the guide and meditation teacher at Wat Buddha-Dhamma at Wisemans Ferry, where he stayed for fourteen years. In 1990, he became interested in the practice of Dzogchen, later becoming a pupil of Namkhai Norbu Rinpoche. In 1991, he disrobed and left Wat Buddha-Dhamma. Two years later he married a Buddhist practitioner from Sri Lanka. They now live in North Queensland, where they have founded a non-sectarian Buddhist centre, Bodhi Citta, in Cairns. They continue to practise Dzogchen.

BUDDHISM EXPLAINED

BY

LAURENCE-KHANTIPALO MILLS

(FORMERLY PHRA KHANTIPALO)

SILKWORM BOOKS

DEDICATION

To all my Teachers of this life beginning with my mother,
Mrs F M Mills and my history master at
Thetford Grammar School,
Mr C G V Tarlor, with these great Masters of the Dhamma—

Venerable Dr. H. Saddhatissa Mahanayaka Thera,
Ven. Kapilavaddo Bhikkhu, Ven. Panyavaddho Bhikkhu,
Phra Dharmadhirarajamhamuni of Wat Sampleung,
Acariya Buddharakkhita Thera of Bangalore,
Urgyen Sangharakshita Mahasthavira,
Dhardo Rinpoche, Dudjom Rinpoche,
Yogi Chien-Ming Chen,
Phra Sasanasobhana, now (1998) Somdet Phra Sangharaja,
Phra Acharn Maha Boowa Nyanasampanna,
Phra Acharn Fun Acaro,
Phra Acharn Singthong,
Phra Acharn Thate Thesarangsi,
Chogyal Namkhai Norbu Rinpoche

I dedicate with devotion all the merits of this small book.

ISBN 974-7100-85-1

This edition first published in 1999 by
Silkworm Books
104/5 Chiang Mai–Hot Road, M. 7, Suthep, Muang, Chiang Mai 50200
Thailand
E-mail: silkworm@loxinfo.co.th

Cover photograph by Pol. Col. Sophon Singhaphalin
Cover graphic by Klik Studio, Chiang Mai
Set in 10.5 pt. Garamond
Printed by O. S. Printing House, Bangkok

01 02 03 04 05   7 6 5 4 3

CONTENTS

PREFACE
TO THE SIXTH EDITION

This book has been brought out by various publishers in Thailand and has now reached a sixth edition. Silkworm Books through the Suriwong Book Centre in Chiang Mai has been authorised by me to publish it. Through some previous editions had photographs these have been omitted in this edition in order to lower production costs. It remains essentially the same book, with additions here and there, as that written by a young monk about thirty years ago. Readers should pardon him for his faults and inexperience. Though I would not now write a book with this structure, perhaps adopting instead a more flexible approach to the Dhamma, still I was somethings surprised when reading through the proofs, to come across familiar explanations of Dhamma which I was using even thirty years ago.

When I consider the book's title however, my ideas have changed. "Buddhism Explained" (in less than 200 pages!) is perhaps rather arrogant! It is certainly so if by 'Buddhism' is meant all the Dhamma's manifestations from Mongolia to Sri Lanka, from India to Japan. In this book though, only the southern Buddhist tradition, Theravada, of Sri Lanka, Burma, Thailand, Laos and Cambodia is explained. Of the varied ways in which Theravada is practised in those countries, the practice in Thailand is emphasised here. As a title though, "Theravada Buddhism in Thailand" certainly lacks the snap of "Buddhism Explained", so the original will be retained. In defence of it, one might plead, 'Well, the basics of Dhamma are the same in all Buddhist traditions', and certainly that is the truth. So while the book cannot claim to explain the particular emphases of the Mahayana Buddhist traditions of China, Korea, Vietnam and Japan or the Vajrayana of Tibet, Mongolia, Nepal and Bhutan, it does thoroughly clarify the foundations of all Buddhist practice. I trust that it will continue to inform readers and lead them to delight in the Dhamma.

I should like to take this opportunity to thank Khun Trasvin Jittidejarak for bringing out this work again, one which has introduced so many to the Buddha's Teachings.

Laurence-Khantipalo Mills
(formerly Phra Khantipalo)
Bodhicitta Buddhist Centre
Redlynch, Cairns,
Australia.

PART I

WHAT DO BUDDHISTS BELIEVE ?

This is a question so frequently asked by so many people newly confronted with the Buddha's Teachings,* especially in Thailand where over 90% of the population declare themselves his followers.

BELIEF IN BUDDHIST TEACHINGS (DHAMMA)

Dhamma is, literally, 'that which supports'; it is the Truth within us. By practising it and by bringing ourselves to accord with it, we can cross over the ocean of troubles and worries. Dhamma is also the formulations of this Truth which we can practise if we are interested to do so. In Dhamma there is no creed and there are no dogmas. A Buddhist is free to question any part of the Buddha's Dhamma, indeed the Teacher has encouraged one to do so. There is nothing which one is forbidden to question, no teaching about which one must just close the mind and blindly believe. This is because faith* in a Buddhist sense is not a blind quality but is combined with wisdom. Thus a person is attracted towards the Dhamma because some wisdom perceives a little truth in it, meanwhile accepting with faith those teachings as yet unproved. Practising Dhamma, one finds that it does in fact work—that it is practical, and so confidence grows. With the growth of confidence

---

* Asterisks occurring in the text refer readers to the Glossary of Pali and Sanskrit words on p. 155.

one is able to practise more deeply, and doing this one realizes more of the truth—so confidence grows stronger. Thus faith and wisdom complement and strengthen each other with practice. In this case, it is easy to see why Buddhist Teaching is symbolized by a wheel, for this is a dynamic symbol.

But one who has seen the Dhamma-truth, being rid of all mental defilements and troubles, an Arahant, has no faith. Such a person having known directly with insight-meditation has something much better: Wisdom.

PRACTISE AND PROVE THE TEACHINGS

From this it follows that the truth of the whole of the Buddha's Dhamma may be proved by oneself in this very life. This is done by earnest practice. The Buddha has assured everyone that they may prove his statements by declaring that his Teaching is something to "come-and-see",* that is, to investigate for oneself, to try it out and see if it works. This may be done since the Buddha was not concerned with speculative theories—these only lead one astray— but with the discovery and teaching of a practical Way of spiritual progress which, "leading inward"* is provable by "each intelligent person for themselves."*

The benefits of practising Dhamma are of three sorts: The first is the benefit to be seen here and now referring to the immediate help that Dhamma practice gives—living becomes easier and problems become lighter while happiness increases. The second benefit is called the benefit to be found in the future. The future may be only tomorrow, later in this life or in other lives but it is sure that 'doing good brings good' (see section on Kamma and its Results). The third of these benefits is called the Supermundane Benefit, the Highest Happiness and the Sublime Peace called Nibbana (see Part III). All of these benefits may be seen by oneself in this life if one has put these Teachings to good use.

DHAMMA AS METHOD, NOT DOCTRINE

This point leads on to another very important distinction between the Dhamma and other religions. The latter have taught doctrines, creeds and dogmas which are not immediately open to proof (or indeed supposed to be proved) but have to be accepted with faith. The Buddha taught methods which one might apply to one's own life and speedily come to see the benefits of their practice here and now. In fact, the whole of Buddhist Teaching is one mass of methods appropriate severally for different times, places and most important, for persons of different temperaments.

As Buddhism is methods or wholesome means, it is true to say that it has no teachings which are not either: based upon, or proceeding towards, Enlightenment.

'Based upon' means stemming from the experience of Enlightenment which made the religious wanderer Gotama into the Enlightened or Awakened One (Buddha, as this a title and not a name). 'Proceeding towards' means that all the Buddha's Teachings are so aimed that anyone who practises them in full may come to experience Nibbana, the Supreme Happiness, the Sublime Peace, the peak of Enlightenment.

THE TRIPLE GEM

In what then, do Buddhists have faith? They have as their highest ideals, the Triple Gem: the Buddha, the Dhamma, and in the Sangha or Noble Order of Enlightened followers. When going to a temple, as in Thailand, Buddhists recite in the ancient Pali language which approaches that which the Buddha spoke, prose passages and verses venerating and praising the Triple Gem. Upon such occasions, they dedicate themselves to follow, to understand and realize inwardly the meaning of Buddha, Dhamma and Sangha. A Buddhist is one who has taken Refuge in or gone for guidance to, the Triple Gem because s/he sees therein the marks of supreme and fearless Truth.

REVERENCE TO TEACHERS

We shall examine what is meant by the Triple Gem in this and the following sections. Meanwhile, mention must also be made of the veneration commonly given throughout the Buddhist world to spiritual teachers, whether they be monks, nuns or lay people. Such teachers are one's Noble-friends,* they give one precious instructions based on thorough study or on realizations hard-won by themselves, showing what is the right way to Freedom.* The posture of respecting such teachers (who for the disciple represent in the present time, the Buddha) and of the images[1] of the Enlightened One himself, is calculated to instill in the mind humility, without which quality, little or no spiritual progress may be made. It is well-recognized in Buddhist psychology that not only does the mind have its effects on the body but also that bodily action affects the mind; they are in fact, interdependent. Hence the care which is taken in this exercise of prostration, the grace with which it is accomplished and the mindful attitude of mind which should accompany it.[2] Three of these prostrations are usually made

1. There is no 'idol-worship' in Buddhism. The figure of Lord Buddha in temples represents to Buddhists some of the qualities of their Teacher and Teaching, it inspires them to recollect those same qualities and so develop them within themselves. The Buddha-figure is also a great aid in meditation and may be used to calm the mind at the time of death.

Also, there is no prayer in Buddhist temples. People do not pray to a Teacher who has attained Final Nibbana over 2500 years ago; they venerate and respect him. The prayer which asks benefits for oneself is quite foreign to Buddhist thought, the latter aiming as it does at realizing no-self.

2. The Buddha is not a god of any sort. When non-Buddhists see followers of the Buddha respecting Buddha-images, they sometimes conclude that these prostrations are made for the worship of, or to implore the favours of, the Buddha. Such is not the case for the Enlightened One himself said that one should be above all pleasure at being wor-

respectively honouring the Enlightened One, his Way to Enlightenment, and those who by their practice of this Way have won the Wisdom and Freedom from mental stains called Enlightenment.

The effective practice of Dhamma, especially its Meditation and Wisdom elements, depends to a great extent upon having a guide whose experience is certainly greater than one's own. Though Buddhist Meditation of some types may be undertaken without a teacher's guidance, it will be many times more profitable if a teacher is available. Thus teachers receive great respect as they are, if both learned and wise, able to give great help to those who study and practise with them.

OFFERINGS MADE IN A TEMPLE

While upon the subject of veneration it might be useful to know the meaning of the various offerings to the Buddha, for it is true to say that Buddhism contains nothing meaningless, or if such practices are found then they are not truly Dhamma.

The three most common offerings: incense, flowers and lights, provide the occasion for a little discursive meditation while they are being offered. While lighting the candle or lamp one reflects: 'Oh, may I become Enlightened* so that I am able to help others.' From that flame, the incense sticks (usually three in number) are lighted with the thought: 'In order to achieve that Enlightenment may the fragrance of my virtue pervade all my actions of body,

---

shipped (or anger at not being worshipped)—in this respect the Buddha has perfect equanimity. Prostrations and all the other respects paid to his representations, are strengthening the wholesome (=good) aspect of consciousness. Prostrating oneself is for the individual's happiness and not for the glorification of a god. The Buddha has no connection with creation myths of the world and is remembered and honoured as a mighty Teacher, greater than any god because transcending those conditions which would lead to becoming such a god. For gods in Buddhist Teaching and the Gods of Theistic religions see below p. 45ff; p. 57 ff.

speech, and mind, as this sweet incense, spreads to all directions.'
Then flowers are offered between joined palms thinking: 'But this
life is short and even though these flowers are fresh and beautiful
today, tomorrow they will be faded and evil-smelling—so it is with
what I call my body.' Thus, in this life which is fleeting and
impermanent, a Buddhist, knowing this, makes an effort to
maintain, indeed to raise the standard of his pure virtue and so take
one step in the direction of Enlightenment.

Buddhists sometimes also offer food and water to the figure of
their Teacher, not of course thinking that he will partake of them
but because, piously, many Buddhists will not take food themselves
until something of the best has first been offered to the Buddha.
The Buddha because the Best among Humanity* merits the best
gifts, and again, it is part of a Buddhist's training to share good
things with others.

The three usual offerings are sometimes taken as symbolizing the
Triple Gem: flowers, particularly the lotus, are symbols of the
Buddha, for a lotus while it grows from mire and muddy water,
rises unsullied above them. Not even a drop of water will stay on a
lotus leaf. Similarly, the Buddha was a Teacher in this confused
world of desires and defilements but he rose above them; he was in
this world but not of this world. Not even the slightest desire
afflicted his mind. This is the symbolism of the lotus. Other flowers
being beautiful remind the devotees of the brilliant and beautiful
qualities of the Buddha's personality. The light which is offered will
then be the Teaching, lighting up all the dark places of the heart
and bringing Enlightenment to replace unknowing. The Order (of
Noble Ones), will in this sequence be represented by the incense,
again because of their perfection which pervades all their actions
whether by mind, speech or by body.

Having given some space to the significance of Buddhist
veneration, it is necessary now to describe in some detail the
meaning of each of these Three Gems separately. However, it
should be emphasized that they are inseparably connected in

practice and attainment. Thus there can be no Dhamma and no Sangha until after a Buddha has arisen in the world. The continuance of the Dhamma depends on the Sangha propagating it, while the Sangha continues so long as there are those who practise and realize Dhamma. It may not be so obvious how the Buddha depends on the Dhamma. This is because whether Buddhas arise in the world or whether they do not, the heart of Dhamma remains forever true. It is commonly described as 'timeless',* there being no time when it first became true and there can be no time in the future when it will cease to be true. Whenever there is sentient existence, this Teaching must necessarily contain the Truth, dealing as it does with the causes of existence—craving and ignorance, and the varied effects of this called suffering or dukkha; and the cause, the Practice-path of Dhamma which when used brings about the results of happiness and peace.

It is true that Dhamma may be temporarily forgotten when it is no longer practised in the intervals between the Buddhas but even when forgotten it is still true and awaits rediscovery. One who does uncover this ancient wisdom in all its fullness and clarity, is said to be a Buddha.

THE GEM OF THE BUDDHA

Who was the Buddha? To answer this question it is not enough merely to take account of one lifetime, for to become a Buddha, the accumulated merits and the liberating Wisdom developed through a series of lives, (see, the section on Rebirth), indeed over vast periods of time, are necessary. The qualities which are needed to effect the final attainment of Enlightenment are called Perfections,* while complete renunciation which is the fundamental necessity can reduce the time of practice to this one life. Upon this are founded the great Purity, Compassion and Wisdom which are characteristic of Buddhahood. In the space available here it must suffice to mention some of these previous births under the appropriate Perfections, and give here an outline of the famous story, so many times related in greater detail, of the life in which the last Buddha, called Siddhattha Gotama, arose in the world.

THE LIFE OF GOTAMA

The child who was to become Gotama the Buddha decided to be born among the Sakyas, a small oligarchic 'kingdom' in what is now the Nepal Terai. His father was the elected ruler of the Sakyas, Raja Suddhodhana and his mother, the Queen, was Mahamaya Devi. It is recorded that at the time of his birth in Lumbini Grove, various unusual occurrences took place portending that the newborn child was indeed a very extraordinary being. All the seers called in by his father, except one, foretold that the infant Prince Siddhattha had two possible careers: to become a world-emperor ruling vast dominions by unswerving justice; or else to leave the household life and, meditating alone, gain supreme Enlightenment thereby showing the Way to countless other beings for their welfare and happiness, this being the prediction of the one seer. While his father who was of the warrior caste, liked the idea of the former career, he did not approve of the latter and made every effort to distract the young Prince from thoughts of renunciation. As he grew up, he received an excellent education and proved to be a brilliantly intelligent student. Besides the study of theoretical subjects, he was given a thorough training in all the martial arts such as would be fitting for a great emperor. Frequently during this time it was noticed by those about him that he took little pleasure in things which the world values highly and that he might often be found sitting alone and with serious mind pondering over the affairs of life. The King's advisers were quick to note this and informed his Majesty of the young Prince's reflective airs. The King therefore determined to keep Siddhattha well-amused within three palaces set in three parks, one each for the hot, wet and cold seasons. In particular, he was never to see a sick person, one grown old, a corpse or wandering monk since it had been predicted that if he did, they would be the cause of his leaving the household life. As soon as the Prince came of age, his father arranged his marriage to Yasodhara, a beautiful maiden of the Sakyan nobility. Thereafter upon the King's orders, Siddhattha lived amidst splendid luxury. His palaces rang with sounds of fair songs sung by equally fair singers. Sweet music sounded in his chambers and went with him into his parks. His apartments were most delicately constructed of costly substances and only the fine and fair among the human race were allowed to enter there. He fed upon the chóicest delicacies and lived close to his beautiful wife and, at his word, anything was done so that he might remain content with worldly pleasures.

But the King had left out of his reckoning one factor about which indeed he could do nothing: that the prince was really a Bodhisatta, one who, ages ago, has dedicated himself to, had raised his thought to one thing—Supreme Enlightenment. A person like this cannot be cajoled into accepting the decidedly inferior pleasures with which sense-desire is associated. So, one day (when he was already nearly thirty), Prince Siddhattha requested his father that he might view his future realm which he had never seen outside the parks. His father deliberated and then ordered a hasty decoration and cleaning of the city. His officers had instructions that the Prince should not on any account see either old people or diseased ones, neither corpses nor monks. However, one by one those dreaded sights appeared to Siddhattha and he understood: Though I am well now, this body is liable to sickness; though I am young and strong now, this body will soon become weak with old age; though I am now alive, this body will surely come to death; and seeing the wandering ascetic, the Prince thought; 'Perhaps indeed that way of life may enable me to understand these pressing questions.' Prince Siddhattha was deeply stirred by these sights and by the problems they raised in his mind. He immediately ordered the return of his once-joyful expedition to his palaces. Not all the dancers, singers, not all the beauties of his palace could break the Prince's earnest reflections.

Soon after, Princess Yasodhara gave birth to a son and when Siddhattha was told of this, he exclaimed, "A fetter has come to me." and so the baby was named Rahula (fetter). Why did the Prince exclaim in this way? Already he was bound by court ceremonial and rituals, while luxuries surrounded him his wife loved him and many retainers depended on him; a son would be another link to bind him to a life which he already perceived was deceptive and distorted the truth. On that same day he resolved that when night had fallen, he would escape from all these bonds and then in freedom, strenuously endeavour to seek the causes for birth, sickness, old age and dying which he clearly saw were the lot of all beings.

That night, after a brief farewell look at his wife and son while they lay sleeping, he set out upon his horse, Kanthaka, accompanied by his charioteer, Channa, into the wild forests which then spread over most of the Gangetic Plain. It was his last ride as a prince upon horseback. Reaching a secluded part of the forest, far away from Sakyan realms, he dismounted, cut off the long tresses of his hair and, giving his rich princely gear to Channa, be donned the patched yellow robes which in the East are the sign of the homeless religious mendicant. Taking a bowl in which to collect offered food, he made Channa return to King,Suddhodhana and inform him what had happened. So well-beloved was the Prince because of his gentleness and consideration for others that many shed tears of deep grief at his departure while his horse Kanthaka, separated from his Master, quickly died of a broken-heart.

The monk Gotama, for such he must now be called, went on his lonely way to seek teachers who would show him the Way to Salvation. Although he studied with two and practised up to the high meditative levels which they had attained he was not satisfied, for the answers he sought to the questions about the world, birth and death were not yet clear to him. It seemed as though something besides ecstatic meditation was needed and so Gotama applied a 'remedy' still popular as a religious discipline in India, that of extreme asceticism. In this great effort to attain Enlightenment he was joined by five ascetics who regarded him as their guru (teacher) and who expected that when he had won the Truth by his mortifications, he would hand on his Truth to them. Thai temple paintings often reflect this typically Indian 'reliance-on-the-guru' attitude by showing the five 'ascetics' gossiping amongst themselves while Gotama, resembling a skeleton sits intent upon his Quest.

This severe practice he tried for six years. He lived in fearful wilds among corpse-fields or in dirty places; he refused to wash and wore no clothes; he lived baked by the summer sun in the day and frozen cold in thickets during winter nights; and he lived on minute amounts of food, systematically starving himself until his fine, once regal, body was reduced to mere skin and bone. In such a way he has taught us that those who aspire for Enlightenment must be ready to sacrifice everything. In order to gain the greatest gain— Supreme Enlightenment, one has to make the greatest renunciation. However, he found that this was only exterior renunciation, only the renunciation of bodily comfort and that by giving pain to the body, the mind was not quietened. Deciding that a lack of inner renunciation of desires was at the root of his troubles, he perceived that bodily strength was necessary to meditate successfully and for that, food would be required. At this decision, the five ascetics who had joined him in his austerities, departed calling him a back-slider for not continuing with these practices. He partook of a meal of rich milky rice pudding and recovering strength gradually went to the famous Bodhi Tree at the place now called Bodh Gaya. It was the Full Moon night of the month of Visakha (usually falling at the end of April or during May). Gotama, a Bodhisatta on the verge of the greatest discovery, sat down upon some grass beneath this tree. He sat in the way countless Indian sages have meditated, with back erect, legs crossed and the hands lying one upon another in the lap. Many beautiful figures of the Buddha in this position are found in Thailand.

The moment drew near for the highest spiritual endeavour. First pacifying the mind by entering upon levels of the concentrations and with a mind alert, he endeavoured to pierce through the gloom of unknowing* and understand the mysteries of existence.

Before this great event could come about, the Bodhisatta had to withstand the assault of the Evil One who, alarmed at the possibility that Gotama might escape his realm of wandering-on* in birth-and-death determined to hinder him in every way within his power. This scene, depicted so often on Thai temple walls shows hosts of demons, animals and monsters attacking, with a full complement of troops, the serene figure of Gotama seated upon a throne far above them. In front of him dance young wantons trying to entice him with their charms. Over all spreads the mighty Tree of Wisdom. This is obviously a symbolic picture although popular imagination regards these events as occurring in just this way. The Evil One and his forces are all those habits, tendencies, the results of past actions in untold numbers of past existences which bind people to certain views and to certain ways of doing things. Gotama, having lived for many lives strengthening the Perfections, now sought not merely to abandon and to thoroughly uproot the remaining subtle tendencies to false views and evil conduct but also to be free from the bonds of conventional goodness. (Having made goodness a strong part of one's character, and weakened evil, one has eventually to relinquish even attachment to the good, for perfect Enlightenment lies beyond all attachments). No wonder then, that he faced turmoil at that time, seeking as he did to pass beyond the bonds of human nature and to discover the Unbounded.

The gathering of all these forces from out of the past did not deter him. With undiminished strength, he rejected the allure of sensual pleasures; he refused to be moved by ancient fears, nor could hatred, anger or dislike be roused in his mind. Then, with a mind calm, settled, and of crystal clarity, he arrived successively at three great knowledges.

The first was knowledge of past lives. It became clear to him how he had been a certain person by such and such a name living in this or that place. From the present life his memory, no longer restricted by the traumatic incidents of birth and the preceding death, stretched back into the last life (where he was a god*—Santussita Devaraja by name), to a life on this earth before that, as Prince Vessantara whose story of unequalled generosity is so well-known and loved by the Buddhists. Back, three, four, ten, twenty, one hundred, one thousand, one hundred thousand lives, through ages of lives until he remembered clearly that distant event when, as the young ascetic Sumedha, he humbled himself before the Buddha Dipankara and made the following vow: 'Oh, may I too one day become a Perfectly Enlightened One endowed with all the powers as you are!' And so on, back and back, past great aeons of cosmic evolution and of devolution, an infinity of lives opened before him for his inspection.

Later that night a second knowledge was gained by him: that of the arising and passing-away of beings according to their intentional action (kamma). Gotama, although not yet a Buddha, was able to perceive that according to whether a being's actions had been predominantly good or evil, so he came to his future birth. He saw how actions in a being's past condition his present mental outlook and how the ways of thinking that he chooses now will in turn affect his future. The tangled web of interrelationships between these three times then became obvious and he saw beings going from dark to light by their good actions, or falling to lower states of birth when they committed evil deeds. This was an insight into intricate meshing of intentional actions and how by them, the results of their own doing, beings place themselves in bondage.

The night drew on. All was hushed as though every creature however small and humble knew of the victory over unknowing which was about to be achieved by one whose fame would then ring down through ages as Gotama the All Knowing One, the Sage of Sakyas.* Before the transcendental excellence of Buddhahood can be found, the prison of unknowing must be shattered. Then with unlimited transcendental insight any problem to which the mind is turned will be understood in all details and without uncertaintly or obscurity. Such an insight is call Destruction of the taints,* for these 'taints' spread themselves, infect, flow into all thought and distort perception. The first taint is that of Sensual Pleasure: desiring always the pleasures of sight, sound, smell, taste, touch and thought while rejecting everything which opposes selfish pleasure, truly a tainted way of living. The second is the taint of Continued Existence: ever craving for life after life, wanting to go on and on, without, of course, wanting to experience the accompanying pain of birth, sickness, old age and death, or the unsatisfactory nature of all sensual pleasures. The third taint is really the fundamental one of Unknowing or rather, of knowing wrongly or partially, of interpreting existence in a muddled way due precisely to the presence of this veil of unknowing in the mind. All these taints were shattered during that night, by seeing their conditioned nature.

That dawn, a fine and clear one, was not just another summer morning but saw the beginning of a new era, of an Enlightened One who had seen the Dhamma in himself and had rediscovered Dhamma for a world of suffering beings. Surveying the world with his Eye of Wisdom he saw that he was most excellent and as there was no teacher whom he might respect as his superior, he resolved to live "revering the Dhamma as my Teacher." Gotama the Bodhisatta, One who was to the world an ascetic and formerly a prince, sat down beneath the Bodhi Tree, but Gotama the Buddha arose from his seat, his mind freed from all obstructions and limitations. The legends relate that all creatures upon this joyful morn lived in peace and harmony, that there was universal happiness.

Though Great Wisdom had been developed to perfection he inclined to the understanding that no one would be able to

penetrate to the Truths that he had uncovered. This disinclination
left him when he used his Divine Eye to survey the world and so
beheld beings rising and falling upon waves of desire in the storm
of existence. Beholding this pitiful sight, Great Compassion blos-
somed like a full-opened lotus in his heart; he saw that there were
indeed a few "with little dust in their eyes" who would understand.
He therefore determined to preach first to his old teachers of
meditation but then learnt that they had died recently; then he
thought of his five erstwhile companions and perceiving that they
were staying in a Deer Park outside Benares, he went to them.

On the way he met a wandering naked ascetic, Upaka, who,
impressed by the fine appearance and serene expression of the
Buddha, asked him who was his teacher and whose teaching did he
profess?

The Enlightened One replied in the following verses, his first
words as a Buddha (according to one account) which mightily
proclaim his Wisdom and are as fearless as the roaring of a lion:

> *Beyond all being, wise to All,**
> *Unsoiled by dhammas* all am I,*
> *Left all and freed by craving's end,*
> *By self I've know, whom teacher call?*

> *There is no teacher here for me*
> *For one like me cannot be found*
> *In the world with all its gods*
> *No one's there to equal me.*

> *Worthy in the world am I*
> *A perfect Buddha, one alone*
> *A teacher truly unexcelled*
> *Cool-become and quenched am I.*

For turning of the Dhamma-wheel
I go to Kasi's city now
Beating the drum of Deathlessness
In the world that's blind-become.

They are Victors who, like me,
Destruction of the taints have won,
By me, are evil dhammas quelled,
Thus, Upaka, Victorious One am I.

                     . Middle Collection, Discourse 26

However, in spite of this Upaka was not ready to receive his Teaching and departed, while the Buddha went by slow stages to Kasi's city to Benares. Near there in the Deer park, he taught his First Discourse, the famous "Turning the Wheel of Dhamma."* The five ascetics became the first Buddhist monks* and all attained Streamentry* upon hearing his words and later became Arahants.*

Then began a long life of teaching and organization in the Gangetic Valley, Gotama was thirty-five at the time of his Enlightenment and for forty-five years thereafter gave the Dhamma to all who wished to hear. He enjoined his Enlightened disciples to go forth and spread the Dhamma "for the welfare of the world, for the happiness of gods and men." Both he and they taught and between them they dispensed the Dhamma to Kings and courtesans, to brahmins and beggars, to high and low alike according to their various powers of understanding. The Order* of Buddhist Monks was established and rules were gradually formed for its internal administration. Likewise an Order of Nuns* was created upon the entreaty of Gotama's foster-mother, Maha-pajapati, who wished to lead the homeless life in company with many other women of the Sakyan clan. Both these Orders were and are open to all who wish to devote their total energies to Buddhist study and practice.

At the age of eighty, Gotama felt that the physical body was worn out and would soon cease to function. Assembling his disciples, he made it known to them that in three months time his Final Nibbana,[3] the passing from all worlds, would take place. This done, he went with a great assembly of monks to Kusinara and there prepared to attain final Nibbana surrounded by disciples, both monks and laity. Those among them who were Arahants who had experienced Enlightenment, did not weep for they knew full-well that all conditioned things, even the physical form of Buddha, are impermanent and subject to decay. But the monks and laity who were still ordinary people* wept bitterly for their Teacher most beloved to them, most precious, compassionate and wise, would soon be gone from them, they would be unable to see him any longer. Yet the Buddha exhorted them in two matters before his final Nibbana: "When I have gone, do not think, 'We no longer have a Teacher', for you should let the Dhamma be your Teacher." And his very last words as he lay serenely between two Sala trees full of sweet-scented blossoms, are a most precious instruction to his followers: "Listen well, O monks, I instruct you: Subject to Decay are all conditioned things: With diligence strive on!"*

As he lay mindfully on his right side, the two Sala trees raining down their sweet-scented blossoms on him, surrounded by worshipping hosts of disciples among gods and men, in tranquillity he passed through the various levels of concentrations* reaching the Nibbana which-leaves-nothing-behind.*

His disciples cremated his remains and reliquary mounds* were set up in many places. The Dhamma continued to spread and this movement was given a great impetus by the famous Buddhist Emperor Asoka more than two hundred years after the Final Nibbana. Buddhism remained for one thousand seven hundred

3. It is not correct to talk about the 'death' of the Buddha for Buddhahood is not the sort of attainment which can suffer death. The body or the physical appearance of Gotama died but a Buddha's state after this happened is not capable of explanation in words. Nibbana is also called the "Deathless State", (see the section on Nibbana lit. 'quenching').

years in the land of its birth, spreading in the meanwhile to Ceylon, Nepal, Burma, Thailand, Cambodia, Laos; Afghanistan, Central Asia, China, Vietnam, Korea, Japan; Tibet, Mongolia, Siberia, and Indonesia. Buddhist 'Messengers of the Teaching' even went as far as Alexandria, Greece and Cyprus in the West and Central America in the East, though these far-separated groups could not thrive for very long. Indian Buddhism after 1700 years had fallen upon decay and was finally crushed by the ruthless Muslim invasions. Everywhere the Dhamma went, it took a fine culture, everywhere it produced superbly artistic symbols, the outward manifestations of the peoples' faith. The reliquary mound or stupa is a particularly characteristic Buddhist symbol and in Thailand splendid examples of it may be found throughout the country particularly at Nakorn Pathom.

REFUGE IN THE BUDDHA

Before passing on to our next subject, Refuge in the Buddha must be examined a little more closely. Some Buddhists, it is true, take Refuge in the inspiring memory of their Teacher, now completely cool ('finally Nibbana-ed') over 2500 years ago. Some have faith that the Buddha Gotama passed to a state beyond words, still 'exists' and can thus be a Refuge. Those with most understanding know that the attainment which the Buddha attained, is open to all who devote themselves to the earnest practice of his teachings. That in fact, every human mind has the possibility to find beneath the ages-old accumulation of rubbish, the jewel of wisdom. In this one may find the most secure Refuge. Did not the Buddha himself say: "Go to no external Refuge?" Thus the last Buddha to appear in this world was Gotama and he inspired his followers both ordained and lay to become as he had become, to model their life and practice on his own since the latter has Supreme Enlightenment as its basis. It was open to anyone, he declared, to observe the precepts, to attain the Concentrations, to cut off the false ego-sense and to blossom

forth in the splendour of Enlightenment. The Buddhas do not set
their followers on a lower level and themselves upon an unattainable
peak of supremacy but encourage them in many skillful ways to
attain what they have attained, as this is something practical
something for each wise person to experience.

THE GEM OF THE REFUGE IN THE DHAMMA

The Refuge in the Dhamma may also be considered in different
ways. Outwardly this is the Dhamma considered as Buddhist
canonical books. There are in three main groups: the Books on
Discipline* of the Orders; the Discourses of the Buddha and his
disciples;* and works of Psychological Analysis.* This literature is
to be found in Pali, a language spoken in Northern India at the
time of the Buddha. Some of these discourses and sayings are also
found in Chinese and Tibetan. The Pali Canon is now nearly
complete in English translation due to the labours of the Pali Text
Society in London (see Appendix III). The collections in Sanskrit
from which the Chinese and Tibetan translations were made have
very largely disappeared through a number of isolated Buddhist
works in Sanskrit have manage to survive. Chinese and Tibetian
Canons are much more extensive than the Pali collections and so
far only small parts of them have been translated. Beside the
collections in Pali, there is a vast, body of literature written as Commentaries, sub-commentaries, guides to the Way and its practice,
an astonishing variety of meditation method described, and so on.
This creative writing, born of practice and showing the Way to
others that they too may practise, is to be found in the common
tongues of every country in which the Dhamma is active. It is
especially abundant in Thailand. While some may take Refuge in
the Dhamma as books, this is not recommended, as veneration of
books without knowing what they contain is far from being
Buddhist Right View.

The real Refuge in Dhamma is taken when it is put into practice and realized. In other words, the Dhamma, as also the Buddha, are really Refuges to be sought within and not in exterior manifestations though the latter may be and usually are very helpful aids for the real Refuge.

As it is our wish to know the Buddhist Teaching, it is obviously necessary to pass beyond this point and examine something of the Dhamma contained in all these collections of books. After that, readers will have gained a little of the knowledge necessary for the Jewel of the Dhamma to be perceived within themselves.

'SUFFERING' AND HAPPINESS

Where then does this Dhamma begin? It has already been mentioned that the Buddha taught everyone who wished to hear according to their powers of understanding. This is important to realize since it involves a very special faculty in the Great Teacher— his Wholesome Means* about which more will be said in the third part of this book. Unless this is taken into account, one who investigates Buddhist Teaching through its scriptures might suppose that there were all sorts of contradictions. It is easy to understand that the Teaching will be different according as it is addressed to a monk or to a layman, to one devoted to the Buddha's Teachings or to an outsider, to intelligent non-committed people or to bigoted brahmins, whether to one who ardently desired to experience final Freedom (Nibbana) or to another with his heart set upon union with God (Brahma) or perhaps rebirth in some lower heavenly state, or as a man.

This last pair, that is, of teachings concerning either final Freedom or the lower goals of renewed human or heavenly existence, is especially important since here are pointed out two fundamentally different attitudes to life, to the practice of Dhamma and the way adopted of dealing with suffering. The first is what may be called the steep path comparable to the direct assault upon the mountain leading up cliffs and precipices and calling for great determination, energy and mindfulness. It is the way to find Freedom or Nibbana in this life, needing renunciation (usually to become a monk or nun since these states of life favour striving) and a well-balanced personality, and lastly and most important of all, a good teacher. This steep way is to be seen in the striving of some Theravada monks and nuns living in forest monasteries, in some Ch'an/Zen monasteries and is a feature stressed also in Tibetan Vajrayana.

The second way is a more leisurely approach to Freedom. It is taking the easiest paths up the mountain without worrying how long it will take to reach the summit. Usually people who adopt this, including the great majority of Buddhists, especially laypeople, do not look for Nibbana in this life-time but by their practice of merit-making, (see II) besides creating happiness for themselves and others in this life, ensure that happiness will follow them also in the next birth, when they hope to be able to take up the task left unfinished in this life.

In what follows therefore, one should bear in mind what has been said of these two courses. They are not, of course, completely separate, for monks and nuns who concentrate on living the Dhamma every moment do not neglect the making of merit, nor of course would it be true to say that the merit-making of layman has no connection with the way of steep ascent. As the path was taught by the Buddha in different ways according to capacity of individuals, so practice should be according to the abilities and requirements of one's character. Having borne this in mind, we may enquire again about the starting point of the Dhamma.

All religions have some starting-point, which in most cases is a set of beliefs formulated in a particular way so as to become a creed. At the beginning of this book it was noted that the Buddha's Teachings have neither dogma nor creed to be believed, so that although it has a very definite direction it is plain that its starting point is different from others. It starts, not from any demand on its followers that they believe, but from the common experience of all forms of life which, in humanity, is sharpened by the increased power of faculties—that of an aching unsatisfactoriness, a knowledge that things are somehow not right and that circumstances ever rolling on, as they are experienced through this body, give no lasting peace and somehow fail to satisfy.

This illness of life which is not so hard to perceive, is called in the Buddha's Teaching—**dukkha**.* (The nearest English equivalent which can compass the wide range of this key term in Pali/Sanskrit is 'Unsatisfactoriness', while 'suffering' is a rather misleading translation. As the former and its derivatives are rather clumsy, dukkha is being used throughout this section). We should briefly consider its symptoms so as to get some idea of how Dhamma, Lord Buddha's remedy, is specially compounded for this disease.

He has declared: **Birth is dukkha**. 'Birth' means the whole process of life from conception to parturition. It is conception which is particularly meant here. Just to be caught up in a situation where one is tied down by bonds of craving to a solid, deteriorating, physical body—this is dukkha. By being lured into birth by craving or forced into it by past actions, one must experience dukkha. Then the whole operation of birth is so painful that if it goes wrong in some way, as modern psychology has discovered, a deep mental scar, a kind of trauma, may be left upon the infant's mind. The Buddha however has declared from his own memories of infinite births, that to be born is a terrifying experience, so much so that most people prefer to forget it. There is another sense in which birth is really dukkha, for in the Buddha's Teachings birth-and-death are different phases of existence from moment to moment. Just as in the body new cells are being produced to replace old ones which are worn out, so in the mind new objects are being presented, examined and dying down. This constant flow goes on day and night, on and on, so that if it is examined carefully (with insight) it will be seen to be an experiential disease giving no peace, ensuring no security, and resulting in no lasting satisfaction. In a moment of experience events arise, exist and pass away but this meaning of birth-and-death is only to be understood with the aid of deep meditation and insight.

Old age is dukkha. This is perhaps more obvious. Teeth fall out, one's nice glossy hair becomes thin and white, the stomach refuses to digest one's favorite food, joints ache and creak and muscles grow weak; more serious than these physical afflictions are such manifestations as failing sight or difficulty in hearing—pages might be covered with them all. Most terrible of all is the mind's declining ability to understand or to react intelligently, the increasing grip of habits and prejudices, the disinclination to look ahead (where death lies in wait) but to gaze back at the fondly-remembered and increasingly falsified past. Lastly, one might mention the softness of the mind which is politely called 'second childhood' and accurately, 'senility'. Not all beings, not all people, will be subject to all of these conditions but growing old surely entails experiencing some of them, experience which can only be distasteful.

Sickness is dukkha. Again, not all will be affected by diseases during life though it is certainly common enough. Consider this body: how intricate it is, how wonderful that it works smoothly even for five minutes, let alone for eighty years. One little gland, or a few little cells going wrong somewhere, marching out of step and how much misery can be caused! Most people, again, prefer not to think about this and so suffer the more when they are forced to face it. To be convinced of the ubiquity of illness one has only to look into hospitals, talk to doctors and nurses, or open a medical textbook. The diseases about which one can learn are enormous in number and fade off into all sorts of nasty conditions for which science has not yet been able to discover the causes. Mental diseases, brought on by a super-strong root of Delusion variously mixed with Greed and Aversion are also included here.

Death is dukkha. Very few people indeed are prepared to die. They want to live longer and longer, a delusion which modern science is making more possible to realize. The craving* for more and more of this life is somewhat toned down, if one believes as many do in Buddhist countries, that this is only one life of a series. Plenty more lives are available to those who crave for them (see I, Rebirth Section), so work begun in this one does not have to be feverishly rushed to a conclusion but may be taken up again in subsequent births. The actual pains of dying are, of course, various and not all people go through physical agonies. But there is distress of another sort: the stresses which are set up in the mind of one whose body is dying 'against his will.' This is really the final proof that the body does not belong to me, for if it did, I could do whatever I wanted with it; but at the time of death although I desire continued life, it just goes and dies—and there is nothing to be done about it. If I go towards death unprepared, then at the time when the body is dying, fearful insecurity will be experienced, the result of having wrongly identified the body as 'myself'.

There follow in the Buddha's description of dukkha, some miscellaneous items which really amplify the above, thus: Sorrow, lamentation, pain grief and despair, are dukkha. These are obvious and no more need be said about them. That the Buddha had to say so much about the above facts indicates how common is humanity's tendency to turn away the head from such things, to use the blind eye and deaf ear when objects warning of these dangers of existence present themselves. This ostrich-like behaviour does not, unfortunately, remove these sources of dukkha.[4] But for the wise Buddhist all these experiences within and without, are recognized as "messengers of the gods," that is, they are indications to arouse Dhamma-practice. All this can be called occasional dukkha.

The Enlightened One continues: to be joined with what one dislikes/ hates is dukkha; and its opposite, to be separated from

4. What has been said here should be sufficient to clear Buddhism of the charge sometimes levelled again at it, of Pessimism. Salvation in Buddhism is aided by a balanced understanding of life in this world and for this, notice has to be taken of suffering. People who have never seen, or do not want to see, dukkha, will not be interested in Dhamma and cannot practise it. Those who know something of dukkha will understand. This is realism.

what one likes/ loves is dukkha. These two conditions are for most people constant companions throughout their lives. Things never seem to be exactly right and either we get what we do not want or lack what we like. The Buddha is pointing out to us here that by following our likes and dislikes, which are after all, endless, we shall not experience a lasting happiness. All we get out of this is further frustration and mounting tension at the opposite poles of greed and aversion. Never can we find, however hard we search throughout all the possible states of being, any stable situation where all unliked things (people, circumstances, etc.) are excluded, and all desired things are present; there is always, if we examine a situation carefully, some fly or other in the ointment.

Not to get what one wants is dukkha. It is a particularly dense delusion which supposes that if all one's wants could be fulfilled, one would be happy. There are a few people who are in the position of being able so to indulge themselves but these, millionaires and the like, are not known to be the happiest of mankind. Such people are able to get what they want materially but what of their bodily and mental conditions? In common with the rest of humanity poorer than they, even millionaires are not able to order, 'Let no worry, trouble, difficulty, disease, old age, death, (or birth) come near me!' These facets of experience are not to be controlled by a large purse, nor by a small one but only by ordering the mind. It is a common experience for the great majority of people not to get what they want. Their desires remain unsatisfied and even when they are able to have what they want, they find that they do not really experience any lasting pleasure. Pleasure from 'wanted' things is transitory (one no longer has the titillation of 'wanting' what is not yet possessed) and in any case objects of desire are impermanent. 'Satisfying' desires through possessing the objects of desire has been likened by the Buddha to a person who drinks salt water to quench thirst. These last three aspects are known as frequent dukkha.

The **Five Grasped-at Groups* are dukkha**. These 'groups' or 'aggregates' refer to a way of analyzing our total personality, that is, into Body, Feeling, Memory/Recognition, Thoughts and Consciousness. To all these we are attached for they have all been grasped when we came to conception. We have grasped human-groups according to the results of our actions (see Kamma and its Results) and identify ourselves not only with the body but variously with the other mental groups as well. Other beings have grasped animal-groups, the groups which exist in a god's life, and so forth but always there is this grasping and clinging tightly to what deludedly we think of as 'me' and 'mine.' This grasping extends through all sorts of life and is the fundamental wrong, the great mistake from which all our various troubles stem. To take a single instance, easily provable, of whether the grasped groups are dukkha or not: Resolve, as soon as you are in suitable surroundings, to sit still for, say, one hour. Just observe what happens: After five minutes a fly settles on your face and you want to brush it off, after quarter of an hour there is an irritation on your leg you want to scratch it; after twenty-five minutes you feel a crick in your neck and want to move it and you may give up after half-an-hour or so when many joints begin to ache, or one's feet go to sleep—or something similar. By jigging around all day and keeping the body in motion, we manage to avoid experiencing the dukkha associated with it (we experience other dukkha instead). Or if you would prefer a more subtle experiment, resolve, when you are in a quiet place, to concentrate all your attention for half-an-hour. Then see for yourself how 'your own' mind wanders against 'your own' resolve. This is a more subtle dukkha. Consider the Buddha though, who could sit down for seven days and without moving, enjoy absolute bliss from his practice of meditation. Much the same is true of many great meditation Teachers now alive, they do not find their bodies or the other groups cause much trouble, but then such sages have removed grasping and clinging from their minds. The dukkha of these five grasped groups is called **continuous dukkha**.

But, one can almost hear readers protest: There are many enjoyable, beautiful things in life! It is true in a relative and limited sense that many things are enjoyable and beautiful (see the section on Inversions). Regarding this, two facts should be considered.

1. Experiences can only be so regarded if one skims over the surface of life without examining it properly. Suppose that you are delighted with the colours and formations of a landscape. "Beautiful" you say, and on the surface it is. But looking for beauty in this way one fails to see the other side of the picture: all the living beings inhabiting that 'beauty' are either the hunters or the hunted. A great, bloody struggle is going on day and night, relentlessly. This is also reality, but it is not beautiful.

2. Pleasure derived from them is **relative** since their arising is dependent on many factors. Enjoying a film depends on electricity, celluloid, a projection camera, its operator, a screen, light, eyes, visual object, eye-consciousness—the list can be continued to infinity. It is **limited** because it begins at a certain time and in certain surroundings and finishes sometime later. The highest type of delight in this world (whatever one variously considers that to be), must therefore come to an end, after which, it being, according to one's preference, the highest pleasure, it must necessarily be succeeded in one's experience by a lesser delight, indeed if not by actual dukkha.

The Buddha has pointed out that whatever is impermanent, that also is dukkha. It is therefore true to say that even our pleasures, as they are impermanent and give no lasting satisfaction while positively increasing our craving for further pleasure, are really dukkha.

It must not be thought that this is all downheartedness, since the Buddha has definite reasons for giving dukkha a prominent place in his Teaching. **First**, it is experienced by all beings without exception and is true for all times and places. **Second**, being part of experience, it is fatally wrong to try to ignore it as most people do. For instance, it just is not done in the best society to converse frankly about death. One would be thought 'queer' or a religious maniac and whenever the subject was broached, silence would fall, people become uncomfortable and make hurried excuses for leaving one's undesirable company. But in Buddhist lands, like Thailand, death and disease are discussed quite openly, acknowledging their existence. **Third**, human beings generally, as indeed all creatures, continually look for pleasure and avoid pain, thus busying themselves in a little, selfish world of their own, which although the effort is really futile, they try to order in the way they desire. **Fourth**, this leads on to a strengthening of the 'I-feeling' and to making more things 'mine' which is just opposite to the way along which real happiness lies. The five groups do not contain any 'I' (soul, self, Self, etc.), and happiness comes from seeing this with insight. **Fifth**, one has to live in the world with others, who have to be considered: How to make them happy? One can never do this while ideas of 'I', 'mine' and all the resulting complications remain as strongly rooted delusions in the mind. **Sixth**, all this dukkha is just unnecessary—there is no need to experience it—if only one will give up craving and unknowing. And as these are of a spiritual magnitude reinforced by an infinity of past lives (see Rebirth) and constantly strengthened in the present by our various desires, so the Buddha has laid out a Path penetrating right into the depths of our hearts, a Path which leads successively through purification by moral observance, mental tranquillity by practice of meditation, and complete emancipation from all bonds such as unknowing and craving, through insight-wisdom. So the Buddha instructs in this way:

> *Not by a rain of golden coins*
> *is found desires' satiety:*
> *desires are dukkha, of little joy,*
> *thus a wise one understands.*

Of paths the Eightfold is the best,
Of truths the Statements Four,
The Passionless of teaching's best,
Of humankind the Seer

This is the Path, no other's there,
for purity of insight.
Enter then upon this Path
bemusing Mara utterly.[5]

Entered then upon this Path
you'll make an end of dukkha.
Freed by knowledge from suffering's stings
the path's proclaimed by me.

Tathagatas* just proclaim the Path
but you're the ones to strive.
Contemplatives who tread the Path
are freed from Mara's bonds.

Dhammapada: 186, 273–76

Out of compassion for ordinary people, Enlightened Ones teach the Dhamma emphasizing dukkha, (while people usually give importance to finding happiness), which will bring the darker sides of life into focus and so develop wisdom in those who want to see and know. Therefore the Buddha has taught the Four Noble Truths which show the sequence of cause and effect in one's own experience. Having in one's heart the cause-craving, one must expect to experience as effects the various sort of dukkha. Having got rid of the cause in one's heart—the destruction of craving, one arrives naturally at the Supreme happiness, Nibbana.

---

5. Mara: the personification of all dukkha, defilements, evil and death.

The Noble Truth of Dukkha, (sometimes translated unsatisfactoriness.) The Noble Truth of the Arising of Dukkha.* (= the 3 kinds of Craving)	Dukkha and its arising
The Noble Truth of the Cessation of Dukkha,* (= Nibbana, q.v.) (happiness) The Noble Truth of the Practice-path leading to the Cessation of Dukkha,* (= the Middle Path of Practice q.v.)	Sukha (happiness) and its arising.

All this may seem very straight forward, the only trouble being that while these Noble Truths are easy to learn, all sorts of emotional blockages prevent us from realizing what they really mean. For instance, regarding the first: we are not aware of the thoroughly unsatisfactory state of much of our life and so do not take the necessary steps to abandon dukkha. And as regards the second: We are already enmeshed in craving, so that to intellectually agree is not enough, we have to start hewing through the bonds. Regarding three: It seems very far away, very remote, and if this is our feeling about Nibbana, it shows how much work we have to do to 'get there' (since Nibbana ultimately is nowhere else but here and now). As to four: the ordinary person finds it possible to practise one or two factors of the Path at a time, such as Right View, Moral Conduct or meditation, whereas for a sage with perfect insight, the observance of the whole Way is natural, no restraints or efforts being needed.

These four Truths constitute Right View and when one has a clear understanding of them, one is said to have "straightened-out one's views." That is, one no longer permits the mind to roam in realms of useless speculation but confronts it with actual experience (dukkha), thus causing an abandonment of the cause (craving) by following the Middle Path of Practice to reach the Cessation of Dukkha (Nibbana).

A lot of the misery experienced in this world can thus be avoided if only one realized for oneself a simple fact: that actions* have their appropriate results.*

KAMMA AND ITS RESULTS

'Actions' or Kammas are what one does intentionally with the body, speaks with tongue, or thinks in the mind. Again, they may be classified as evil in intention or good. 'Evil' here means debasing one's mind or production of harm to other beings and therefore unwholesome; 'good' means actions conducive to the development of one's mind or to others' happiness and therefore wholesome. Generally, Buddhists avoid the use of 'good' and 'bad' and prefer to talk instead of the categories of 'wholesome' and 'unwholesome' action,* as we shall do henceforth.

To expand a little on the above categories: it is actions of the mind with which we are concerned here, since mental action is fundamental to verbal and bodily action. Whether an action is intentional or not is very important in Buddhist practice. Actions which are willed, deliberate, accompanied by volition, are kamma; these are potentially productive of a future result. Other deeds which are unintentional do not bring about any future result. To illustrate this: supposing a mosquito settles on a person's arm and s/he, not liking such an insect, raises a hand and kills it—such is an intentional action and therefore kamma with a potential result. But the person who lies down and unknowingly crushes a mosquito on the pillowcase, has done so without intention—thus this action is without future result. What has been said here about killing applies also to any other harmful action and also to beneficial ones. Thus a person who intentionally venerates the Buddha may expect a good result from that action, whereas a child who copies that adult's actions but does not know their significance and consequently does not perform it intentionally, has no result to expect from it.

As to results, they are as one might expect: if unwholesome seed is sown now, a crop of painful results can be expected in the future; and conversely, wholesome actions are productive of pleasant, happy results. From thistle-seed we should not expect a crop of fine apples, so it is very important what kamma we initiate in the present, for our future weal or woe is to a large extent dependent on our present. One person, intent only on the accumulation of more and more wealth regardless of the feelings of others, even in this life may develop miserliness in mind, often reflected by a grasping countenance. Another, sincerely concerned with a religious quest will also develop a mind and outward features reflecting their particular concern. Thus, we should always be aware of whether our minds are pursuing wholesome or unwholesome matters for even in this life the fruits of kamma can be seen. In this way arise a great number of the many differences between beings in the world. Inequalities too obvious to need further comment are seen amongst mankind—rich and poor, clever and dull, wise and stupid and so many more. If these inequalities are great then what of the animals? Kamma and result operating through the three times of past, present and future, account for many of these differences.

Results are various as to the time-interval between the commission of the kamma and their appearance. Some kammas have an immediate result and the relationship may be perceived readily. Others fruit after some time, and it is more difficult to see the connection, yet others do not come to fruit in this life but in the next or in more distant future lives. These are most difficult to understand, and indeed, unless the power of remembering former existences is developed by the practice of meditation, the ordinary person has no way of understanding events which to him are either inexplicable, thought of as random or chance occurrences, or put down when all else fails, to such enigmatic factors as 'the Will of God.'

Kamma and result is a practical teaching to be seen in one's own life and to a limited extent in others. Why does intentional action produce a result? In such action there is an expenditure of energy much greater than occurs with unintentional action. That energy may be called 'will-power' though this is not a Buddhist term. It is well-known in the physical science that energies expended are productive of some resultant effect. Due to the expenditure of will-energy a result may be expected to arise some time after the kamma, depending on the presence or absence of conditions which aid or retard its fruition. The formula which is used for this Dependent Arising* is: 'X factor' being present, 'Y factor' arises; 'X' not being present, 'Y' does not arise. The kamma is said to be a seed planted in the soil of the mind-continuity which, when conditions are right, will germinate. Characteristic tendencies are built up. This is the accumulation of conditioning agents which were laid down in a past life becoming largely "subconscious" in this one. When accumulated in this life, they become patterns for the future.

This stream of interrelated events flows on through the three periods of time: past actions condition present character and environment to a greater or lesser extent. As the past strongly conditions the present life, ability to choose in the present moment is limited. When there is more freedom from past conditioning, freedom of choice in the present becomes greater.[6] The sage well-skilled in Virtue, Collectedness and Wisdom, is free of conditioning from the past and, though such a one may still experience results of past kamma, choice in the present is unlimited. Most people are swayed to a greater or lesser extent in their choices, a fact to be remembered, as present, willed actions condition future existence. Moral

6. It is sometimes said that Buddhism is 'fatalism'. Nothing could be further from the truth. It is true that we must experience the fruits of past kamma which certainly limits and influences our choice in the present. But it is in the present when we make our decisions, wholesome or otherwise and when if we take matters in hand instead of allowing them to over power us, we can for instance decide to train ourselves in this or that way. The religious life in Buddhism is not one of sitting down and resignedly letting whatever must be, happen. There is no room here for concepts of fate, doom or destiny. The Buddha urged his followers many times to make an effort, to strive diligently and this can be done only in the present moment.

responsibility is thus firmly established in Buddhist Teaching where one who practises, knows:

"I am owner of my kamma, heir to my kamma, born of my kamma, related to my kamma, abide supported by my kamma. Whatever kamma I shall do, whether good or evil, of that shall I be heir."

Only I receive the fruits of kamma made by me; other people cannot receive my fruits, nor I the fruits of others:

> *"By oneself doing evil,*
> *does one defile oneself,*
> *oneself not doing evil,*
> *one purifies oneself;*
> *purity, impurity depend upon oneself,*
> *no one can purify another."*
>
> Dhammapada 165

Readers will have noticed that this explanation does not mention "sin", a concept alien to Buddhist thought. A Buddhist who breaks the Precepts (see II, virtue), knows that results will be experienced sooner or later according to those actions and therefore renews the Precepts, resolving to strive to keep them pure in future. Such a person is not weighed down by a great burden of guilt, the latter being a very unwholesome mental attitude productive of future sufferings. Kamma which has been made cannot be unmade or washed away through faith or rituals. Wholesome or unwholesome, the fruits of it will be borne by the doer sooner or later. Only the Buddhas and enlightened disciples break the bonds of kamma. It is said that kamma which has been made does not wear out, even in the course of aeons. The potential just awaits the right conditions to come to fruit.

But kamma, however "heavy" it is (on the side of evil, the murder of human beings, especially mother and father; on the wholesome side, the attainment of the four concentrations), is certainly finite. Since the actions, the causes are finite, which are the fruits or results of these actions, must also be finite. No infinite state of existence is possible since kamma is never infinite in extent. Heavenly existence must flicker to a close and the torments of the hells must be quenched for all beings bound to the Wheel of birth and death.

REBIRTH (literally: Again-being)*

Reference has been made already to lives previous to the present one which an individual may call to mind if the mind is cultivated correctly. The Buddha and many of the great great sages in his tradition have remembered past existences and seen, moreover, how kamma initiated in one life has come to fruit in another.

This teaching of a continuity of lives is not peculiar to Buddhism but is accepted also in Hinduism, Jainism and the religion of the Sikhs. It has for long been a strong undercurrent, though not officially accepted, in Islam (Sufism), Christianity (Origen and the Gnostics) and is well-known in Neo-Confucian and the Taoist teaching.

Obviously, a teaching in which birth depends on intentional past actions (kamma) makes some sense. It gives value to life and brings a sense of justice into what might well seem a chaos of injustice. If one wants to know how evil-doers can be happy and wealthy, while good people groan oppressed in many ways, this too is answered by the teaching on kamma and rebirth, for as has been said already, not all intentional actions have immediate fruits.

Not only has the teaching on rebirth a value for those who would see some justice in this world, it also has a pragmatic application. When he was teaching those who took rebirth for granted, the Buddha strengthened their belief, while others who were sceptical and questioning, instead of asking them to accept rebirth, he employed a 'wager argument'. In this way he focussed on the practical benefits of this teaching, here and now. These are two: concerning the past, and regarding the future.

Thus, supposing that pre-existence is true and that my present sufferings are resultants from misdeeds in past lives (where they cannot be traced to misdeeds in this life!), acceptance of suffering, such as serious disease, is made much more easy and the afflicted person does not have to grow bitter thinking, "Why has this got to happen to ME?" It is also a great incentive to strive now to keep the Precepts and to develop the mind by way of meditation. Suppose that I have been treading the wheel of rebirth for an infinity of time and is this not a spur to do something about it in this life?

Again, supposing future existences are to be my lot, I would be a foolish person indeed if failed to provide for that future! If one could be certain of progress in higher states from life to life then one might sit back comfortably, but the truth is that the future lies in one's own hands. Whether or not rebirth exists, nothing is lost by living a good life here and now, unblamed by others. Seeing enough of dukkha in this world and possessing understanding of its significance urges one to scale the prison walls of birth and death.

We shall therefore assume just on these pragmatic grounds that there have been past lives and that there may well be future existences too.

A succession of lives with a soul incarnating into a series of bodies is often called reincarnation. In Buddhism, the teaching regarding this matter is fundamentally different and we refer to it here as rebirth.[7] Literally, this is "again-being," a rather unwieldy word

---

7. There is no reincarnation in Buddhism because there is no unchanging spiritual entity, no soul can ultimately be found which can reincarnate. Buddhism does not make a dichotomy of the perishable body on the one hand and an eternal soul on the other. The Buddha's insight discovered that both mind and body are interrelated and continually changing streams of events in which no unchanging soul or self as an ultimate principle, can be found. How rebirth is possible without such an entity is outlined in the paragraphs following.

which does preserve, however, the dynamism of this Buddhist Teaching.

Everyone will agree that the body changes from hour to hour, minute to minute, constantly wearing out and being replaced. If one pauses for thought, the same will be found true of the mind, that is, it will be seen to be a stream of mental words and images forever flowing on. It is therefore easy to understand intellectually the impermanence of both mind and body. What then of the "soul"? Here one should distinguish the common conception of "I-ness" felt by everyone regardless of their views, from the speculations of the theologians constructing a system in support of their views on the basis of that feeling of "I-ness". Now both these views, natural and sophisticated, are based upon the all-inclusive classification of our character as Five Groups (see above, on dukkha). The innate **feeling** that one has a soul, is the Feeling Group. **Views** about the soul are the Thoughts Group. These Groups are impermanent so there is no ground for assuming the existence of an unchanging entity or soul. Such an assumption is condemned in the Buddha's Teaching as merely empty speculations based upon craving but having no basis when explored by Wisdom.

But according to relative truth, the "I" exists: there is a continuity which progresses from day to day and which I and others identify by such and such a name. Still, upon reflection, the "I" which existed when I was three years old (my photograph at that age showed a small and sulky podge of a face), and that which is now sixty-odd, bear little resemblance to each other and while they are obviously not completely different people, it is equally obvious that they are not the same. Here, we have another illustration of the law: "X" factor being present, "Y" factor arises—dependent on the existence of that small boy of three, the present man of sixty has come to be. This process of Dependent Arising not only goes on from one moment to the next but also applies from the death of "one individual" to the rebirth of the succeeding one. Thus dependent upon a certain being in a previous life, this being has come into existence, those two having the relation to each other of "neither the same nor different".

How does this process of rebirth actually work? If a person near to death is questioned, it will often be found that s/he does not desire death. No, s/he **wants** only to live—there are the spring cabbages to plant, the neighbour to talk to, a nephew from a distant town to see, another book to be read, and so on, and so on. There are so many things to be done that very few are really prepared to die gracefully and, relinquishing all worldly matters over which they can no longer have any say, come to death and their future existence in an accomplished manner. A person who, though at death's door, has a head full of worldly concerns, craves for sensual pleasures and further existence (becoming) in the sensual realms. One who dies with the blessings of heavenly existence in mind really looks forward to these other-worldly delights and therefore has craving for being in a heavenly state. In either case there is the desire for future life.

This desire for further life, raised to the point of desperation as the various senses fail and the body ceases to function properly, is accompanied by the unexpended force of much kamma, the fruits of which have yet to be experienced.

The mind at the point of death may perceive different signs: which are either symbols out of the past or those presaging the future. A symbol representing some event of the past life may be seen, (a wedding-ring symbolizing marriage, or a rice-bowl representing generosity in giving food), or a picture-memory of some occurrence during that life may also be seen. These symbols have a great influence on the next life and one dying with an unwholesome memory-symbol or picture as the object of consciousness (as a person who remembers some fraud s/he has committed, the bad words used to revile another, or a murder) is bound for a rebirth in accordance with that consciousness. As the latter is connected with the unwholesome, so the birth will be unpleasant. On the other hand, dying inspired by thoughts of religious faith or recollecting the wholesome meritorious deeds one has performed, leads to rebirth in a realm where the wholesome predominates—i.e. in the happiness of what is called 'heaven'. Immediately after death of the physical body, while possessing a mind-made body, one may see a man and woman making love and be attracted to them, only to find that one is now entangled and must suffer womb-existence and eventual birth.

These kinds of consciousness are known together as 'relinking consciousness'* and according to their nature, so is the birth to be experienced. Relinking consciousness is a resultant or fruit of past kamma.

So one goes according to one's deserts and, as existence in pleasant states and those unpleasant is alike impermanent, so birth follows birth, sometimes enjoyable, sometimes painful, sometimes middling. Dependent on the life of a previous 'individual', this present being has come to existence; depending upon the kamma now of this present being, so a future 'person' will come to be. 'I,' in the present, am neither the same as that past being, nor different from it, but depending on it, 'I' have come to exist now. So the continuous stream of existence* rolls on.

The question is often raised: 'Why is it that if I had a past life or lives, I do not remember them?' This is well answered by illustrations of the power of memory. First, do you remember from minute to minute exactly everything which happened yesterday? Memory, the third of the Five Groups, being so defective that even a negative answer to this question must be given, why should one remember events which may have happened many years ago? Again memory, as one support of the ego-sense, only registers certain events, forgets others and distorts even the information which is retained. Ask an old person what the weather was like when they were young and they will be sure to declare that it was better than it is now, and that crops were better, summers longer, rain more plentiful, and so forth. Meteorological records will prove them wrong—the weather was then much the same as it is now but memory has conveniently forgotten the unwelcome rain or the bitter cold and looks back in fact, upon an imaginary 'golden age'. It is a feature of the human memory to remember the happy and forget the unhappy thus building up a distorted picture of the world. One particularly painful experience which is soon forgotten and then overlaid by subsequent sense-experience is the memory of being born. This is an excraciating experience for the child as Buddhist psychology has always taught and modern obstetrics recognizes. Preceding this, comes existence in the womb which, far from being a safe and comfortable retreat as some psychologists aver, is a dreadful time for the embryo, which is not merely the very first beginning of a physical organism, but is a being often possessed at that time of memories as yet undimmed of a former existence, perhaps one much more pleasant than the prison-like surroundings in which it now finds itself. Further back lies the moment of conception for which the Buddha has taught that not only the physical particles from male and female are needed, but also the being (with a mind-made body) seeking rebirth.

As we are speaking of events which prevent most people remembering previous lives, it only remains to add the agony of dying to the other pains set forth above and it will be readily understood that few indeed will wish to remember so many events of a traumatic intensity and most will hurry to forget.

A few, however, do remember. Many children, many more than is usually supposed, do have recollections of their past lives. Some are also born with bodily markings which are the result of some action in the past existence. A few adults retain these memories quite clearly but they often become dimmed by the developing faculties of mind while growing up. Some cases of such memories have been collected in Thailand and with many cases from other countries, are being investigated by Dr Ian Stevenson of the University of Virginia's School of Medicine. In many of these cases it is possible to check the details remembered with the aid of living people or past records, and a high degree of accuracy is a remarkable feature of these memories. Deep hypnosis also sometimes produces details of a previous existence thought not always the last one. Finally, and most dependable of all, are the memories awakened through a mind clear and concentrated in meditation when as we have seen, not merely one life may be recalled, but even countless ages of lives may be reexperienced in complete clarity of detail.

Summing up this section on rebirth may be done in the words of a famous Buddhist simile from the questions asked by the Indo-Greek King Milinda (Menander in Greek) of the Enlightened monk Nagasena: Rebirth is by the latter compared to the changes which a single jug of milk may undergo. To begin with there is just milk, this separates to cream, this turns to butter, from butter comes ghee and from ghee, the skim of ghee, and such processes may develop on from another, infinitely. Each stage is compared to one birth and all the time from the stage of being milk until it becomes ghee-skim, there is no underlying entity which actually goes unchanged—there are here only processes at work, unstable processes in the process of further change.

LEVELS AND PERCEPTIONS

Having dealt briefly with Rebirth and how one is reborn, two further questions require answers: Where does birth take place? and why is one reborn in such realms?

Before answering these questions some points may be considered. Notice that the first question is concerned with spatial position, asking the question 'where'. It is most important to understand this 'where' properly.

If one first takes the question, 'Where am I living now?' the solution to the problem of rebirth becomes easier. Assuming the relative truth of the concept 'I' or 'myself' and concentrating on where-living-now, the answer can only be: On the human level of the mind related to a human body, the two being bound together by the intentional action (kamma) of the past. I am therefore called a human being and consider myself as such.

Now there are occasions in my life when I am liable to become other than human. When I am in a great rage my human perception is quite upset and it is quite possible that people may say of that furious-I: "Did you see his face? Like that of a demon!" Perhaps the situation worsens to a deranged-I who sees the most fearful and horrible sights and suffers intensely—and then where am I living except in one of the hells?

Other degenerations from human level are possible. Lust may drive me on to act like an animal or worse than an animal. The I which delights in porn, whatever effort at justification, is just an animal-I. Or again mean people behave like hungry ghosts even in this life while the quarrelsome could be compared to titans. Nor are gods outside the range of mind. Here in this life may be seen those, variously honoured as saints, rishis and the like, in whom the divine states of mind are manifest.

All these are to be seen—where? As possibilities of the mind. All these, from the loftiest abodes of Brahma to the most terrible depths of hell do not exist unless there is the kamma which produces experience of them.

Rebirth into different realms may thus be regarded in two ways: either as rebirth at the end of this life with which idea we are fairly familiar, or else as rebirth following death which takes place from moment to moment, so that in this very life from day to day, we may range about through states of mind equivalent to the realms of gods, or be dragged down into the pit of hell.

Since mind (or continuity of 'minds' would be better) is a stream of actual and potential forces, the evolution or degeneration of which takes place in this lifetime, it does not pause when the death of the physical organism takes place but flows along in the channels (or patterns of thought) which are made in the present.

Usually in Buddhism either five or six different realms of existence are described as possible bourns though these by no means constitute a rigid system, as experiences within each of them vary enormously, varying according to the past kamma of the beings living in them. Of these, only two, those of humanity and animals, are normally perceptible to human beings. Before we shrug our shoulders at the existence of invisible beings in states unknown to us,[8] we must consider one thing: the relativity of perception.

We perceive the world only in the particular range of experience to which humanity is limited. One is human because of past intentional action (kamma) and one has the sense-organs (including mind) of humanity for the same reason. These are the fruits of former actions.

Normally, people assume the world 'out there' exists just as they perceive it (by way of eye, ear, nose, tongue and physical contact) but if we consider these sense organs, it must be apparent to us that the world 'out there' is really dependent on our particular modes of perception. For instance, the human eye limits and conditions by its very structure the objects we are able to see. It is well-known that a bee can see, as a colour, ultra-violet but we have no idea of how to describe it. It follows therefore, that if our sense organs were differently constructed, our world 'out there' would also be quite different.

In the Dhamma the mind (or heart) is regarded as a sixth sense, having as its objects ideas and memories. 'Mind', really a congeries of mental and emotional processes, working in our case usually upon the human level, conditions all our perception from a human point of view.

8. This is like a man with the smallest power transistor radio able only to pick up stations in Thailand, who upon being told of Australian, British or American stations, just laughs and declares that his little radio receives all possible stations. A person with a really powerful set knows that he is wrong. Human beings so proud of their mental capacity, seldom like to admit that they could possibly be limited: the skilled meditator with so much more experience of the real range of existence, knows how small is the range of the unpractised mind.

One's attitude to these realms at the moment not directly perceived, should rather be the open mind. One does not close the door of one's mind nor does Buddhist Teaching demand that one shall accept them without question: until, and if, they become a part of one's experience one just maintains an open mind regarding them.

Thus understanding the relativity of the six sense organs—eye, ear, nose, tongue, body (touch) and mind, and the consequent relativity of perception, it is not difficult to understand that all the realms besides being actual and potential in our own situation, are also all present here-and-now as far as beings in those other realms are concerned. The idea of heavens in the sky or hells under the earth is taking literally and as cosmography what is really a psychological truth. Superiority and inferiority certainly apply to the experiences of beings in the various realms mentioned in the next few pages but the truth is that they all exist as interpenetrating realms just here. To explain how this can be let us quote a famous Buddhist verse by the great Teacher, Nagarjuna:

> As a water-vessel is
> Variously perceived by beings:
> Nectar to celestials,
> Is for a man plain drinking water,
> While to the hungry ghost it seems
> A putrid ooze of pus and blood,
> Is for the water Serpent-spirits
> And the fish, a place to live in,
> While it is space to gods who dwell
> In the sphere of infinite space;
> So any object live or dead,
> Within the person or without-
> Differently is seen by beings
> According to their fruits of Kamma.

Our world, viewed in the light of this teaching, suddenly becomes endowed with great mystery. All around us, wherever we are and however ordinary our life and situation seems to be, other beings are rejoicing in heavenly pleasures, or may be dwelling formlessly in vast limitless contemplation, crying miserably for want of sustenance, or perceiving and feeling the fearful tortures of hell.

These beings' perceptions, differing and limited by kamma as ours, are seldom able to be aware of other beings dwelling in other states.

However, in the case of a few people, their minds are not so limited and they are able to penetrate into other realms. The most reliable way of doing so is by means of a mind skilled in meditative concentrations accompanied by full awareness, or as Buddhists usually say, mindfulness; such a person is able, at will, to experience some or all of the levels of existence which are about to be described. A few of the lower existence levels are also open to mediums of the spiritualist tradition but as their experiences are accompanied by slothful mental states, it is unwise to place much confidence in their pronouncements.[9]

REALMS OF EXISTENCE

There are the following six realms, mapped out from the experiences of the Buddha and his Enlightened disciples, beginning with the superior and progressing 'downwards', into which one may be 'born' according to one's kamma.

The Gods (deva, literally: **Shining Ones**). The Buddha and many other religious teachers have had contact with beings more mighty, long lived and happy than humanity. They enjoy various states of existence which accord with the different levels of mental development which are open to cultivation by human beings.

Thus a person decides to spend life developing meditation. Doing

9. A medium (provided there is no fraud) may gain contact with a number of ghostly personalities who often, as we shall see, exist upon a very low level. Mediums may occasionally contact some of the lower gods from the lowest heavens—those of sense-desire. From the first they will only get incoherent babble (which is often 'interpreted' for the comfort of supposed relatives), but from the gods more meaningful messages may be derived. However, Buddhism discourages mediumistic practices as harmful to those who if they are seeking rebirth, should be free to go forward to a new existence and not be dragged back to old ties, which they cannot contact or live with any longer. To awaken old cravings in them is but to torment them.

this, one can reach the level of the Formless attainments.* Becoming proficient in these (a very rare thing indeed) one is able to die with the mind dwelling on one of the four Formless levels. Dying in this way, the mind continues to exist on that level. Conventionally we may say 's/he has been reborn in such-and-such a Formless Realm,' but it is nearer to the truth when put thus: 'That continuity which on earth we knew as So-and-so, has now arisen (not 'born' as there is no physical birth amongst the gods) in such-and-such a Realm.' The gods of the Formless Realms abide in their respective states of Infinite Space, Infinite Consciousness, Nothingness, and Neither-perception-nor-non-perception, for periods of time almost impossible for us to conceive. It is hardly true to say that they 'enjoy' their enormous life-spans, for they are beyond enjoyment in the ordinary sense of the word, since their attainment is founded upon equanimity. Yet, when the merit from the earthly practice of the Formless Attainments has been exhausted, they can no longer abide in that sort of existence and 'fall' to rebirth in spiritually lower Realms usually amongst the gods of the Form Realms, next to be described.

Buddhist practice does not particularly encourage the attainment of these Formless Realms, for as meditations they are apt to be something of a spiritual 'No through road', except in the hands of a meditative genius who may use them with good effect. As states of existence they are rather cosmically isolated and to get 'stuck' therein (not perhaps the fate of many people) is to cut off all hope for a very long time of developing Wisdom and so of Nibbana. One may, for instance, miss the chance of hearing many Enlightened Ones teach Dhamma through arising in these realms of long existence.

More spiritually fruitful are practices which lead one to experience the worlds of Form. By attaining the four Concentrations* described in Buddhist texts, one is able to experience the different worlds of Subtle Form which correspond to them. The gods which arise in these worlds (in the same way as the Formless gods), have fine-material bodies and enjoy spiritual pleasures. Whereas the basic emotional tone among humans is one of sensual pleasure, among these gods it is one varying from Loving-kindness to spiritual Equanimity (for the way to these Heavens of Form, see II, the Divine Abidings). The practice of the Divine Abidings, Loving-kindness and the rest, overcomes the grosser desires, particularly for sex. The gods of subtle form, (and of formlessness), therefore, have risen above the gross duality of sexual differentiation. Nor do they know conflict, since the cause for this sense desire, is not found among them. Their lifetimes are less enormous than the preceding but still colossal by earthly standards.

Among them there are some gods who are proud of their state and have the belief (due to their prior arising in the realm which they inhabit), that they are: "Victor, Unvanquished, All-seeing, Controller, Lord, Maker, Creator, Chief, Disposer, Master, Father of all that has become and will be." The Buddha had cause to counsel such gods on several occasions and to point out that far from being Eternal, they were essentially, like all other living beings, impermanent, having had a previous life and very likely to know a subsequent existence too.

According to the Buddha's Wisdom, beings who think of themselves as Eternal Creators are themselves deluded. They have in past lives, practised much meditation and thereby become great even among the gods but they do not remember their past existences, nor have they gained much Wisdom (or they would not be where they are). Other gods deceasing from the supposed Creator's company come to birth as human beings and, practising meditation, gain a memory of their previous life but not of others preceding it. With deep conviction they come thus to believe that this or that god whom they remember clearly, is the Maker of Heaven and Earth, etc. On this basis of incomplete knowledge, they then set out to proclaim, fired by their inner experience, a salvific message to the world. It is thus that five hundred of one thousand years respectively before the major theistic world faiths came into existence, the Buddha from his Wisdom gently pointed out the origin of such religions.

There are also many gods who questioned the Buddha and were taught by him during his meditative retreats among them. Many became his disciples and still live perfecting themselves and instructing others in these Realms of Form. With these meditative concentrations as a basis, or abiding as a god in them, Wisdom may be developed if the right counsels are available. In this way such a life may be fruitful. After spending a long existence there, if release from the round of rebirth is not won, the next birth will usually be either among the lowest group of gods (see below), or again as a well-endowed human.[10]

A person who leads a blameless moral life and makes merit (see II) and perhaps does a little meditation (without attaining any of the concentrations), has raised the mind in quality above the run of ordinary people but has not yet broken through the barrier of sensual desire. At death, such a mind dwelling with calm joy upon a life beneficent to other beings, arising (rebirth) takes place in the Heavens of the Realm of Desire. There are several different levels here where subtle sense pleasures may be enjoyed. Amongst the gods of these planes there are both male and female between whom there is a sort of refined heavenly love.

In general, the common Hindu, Christian and Muslim ideas of Heaven or paradise correspond to these states, which are described as abounding in jewels and gold, shining and full of melodious sounds. Life in them, no doubt very delightful, is shorter than existence among the higher gods. There are fewer beings in these states who are able to comprehend the Truths taught by the Buddha since they are too much attached to having a delightfully pleasant

10. The highest heavens of theistic religions are equivalent to the Realms of Form and certainly the beings there have immense merits and a very long life. However, the western group of religions aver that one of these Brahmas is the Creator and worship him, while in Buddha-dhamma it is recognized that all beings, however great they are and just because they exist, must be impermanent.

time to be able to listen to, or practise, the Teachings on Wisdom. In Buddhist tradition, however, one of the heavens is the abode of the future Buddha who is called Ariya Metteyya (Maitreya), the Loving One. He is now a Bodhisatta in his last life but one and awaits suitable conditions to take birth at last upon this earth, gain Perfect Enlightenment, and then show the Ancient Way, the Dhamma shown by countless past Buddhas, as by Gotama Buddha in the present, to yet more people in that future time.

To conclude our very limited account of the gods, the ancient simile of the Pali scriptures will illustrates their position. 'Birth' among them is compared to the experience of a weary traveller on a hot day coming at last to a luxurious palace in which upon an ornate divan covered with costly materials, that person is able to rest and experience feelings which are exclusively pleasant.[11]

The Titans.* The last-mentioned beings were the gods of the Sensual Realm, and in this realm all the remaining types of birth occur, where, as we have seen, due to the presence of sense-desire there must always be a certain degree of conflict. This is so even among these gods for as they have desires, albeit for more subtle pleasures than humanity usually craves, so they have to battle against war-like beings, said to have been originally gods but driven out of the heavens because of their quarrelsome nature (compare the fall of Satan and his hosts). These beings, who may be called titans, are possessed of great power but are quarrelsome, jealous and injure themselves. Theirs is a world of power and bitterness, a strange and terrible combination.

11. It is sometimes said that Buddhism is 'atheistic' or a 'godless religion'. What has been said above should disperse this notion or rather correct it. The gods may be worshipped for limited and worldly blessings but being impermanent and worldly themselves, they cannot grant prayers concerned with that Freedom (Nibbana) which is Supermundane and which they have not gained. The lesser gods are somewhat equivalent to angels except that according to Christian mythology, one cannot become an angel. Buddhism is only atheistic in the sense that it rejects as false the theory of a First Cause, a Creator God.

How is this type of birth related to human existence? Suppose a person loves power and spends their time securing a hold over others. Such a person loves best to give orders even if they result in hurting others; they scheme, plan, plot and do not hesitate to remove rivals by violent means. A mind like this set on gaining power during life, is not able to relinquish the power-lust when death comes. Dying with the thought of retaining that power over others such a person comes to birth among the titans, where certainly there is power—but all the other titans have it too! All those who have power but misuse it are heading towards this titan-birth. Not at all a pleasant arising.

Human beings.* Next in the scale comes humanity. In the Pali simile, the human state is described as follows: a person travelling along a certain way comes to a large and shady tree with comfortable flat ground beneath it; there s/he takes rest and experiences feelings which are **abundantly pleasant**. The gods and humanity are said to enjoy 'happy' conditions whereas the titans and the three other types of births described below are decidedly 'unhappy.'

We occupy a very important place in the Buddhist cosmos, because we have the power of decision. Human life is a mixture of the happy with a good dash of the bitter. When experiencing this mixture we will not always be lulled into a sense of false security by too much pleasure and, having the great advantage of being fairly intelligent, we are capable of doing something about our woes.

By contrast, the gods live lives graded up from the super-pleasurable through radiant bliss up to a rarified equanimity with habitats being so calm and enjoyable that they do not often take an interest in actively developing factors leading to the Supermundane, (except when aroused by a Buddha or other great sages). They are also living rather on spiritual credit and are therefore limited in ability to make unusual decisions such as to pursue actively a religious quest. The titans are too much preoccupied with brawling and wounding to practise a Path. In the other three births, the hungry ghosts are concerned only with unsatisfied cravings, the animals have minds centred upon food and sex, while the unfortunate hell-wraiths are too much tormented in innumerable ways even to think about the Path.

Humans can, and occasionally do think about it. Less often they actually put Morality, Collectedness and Wisdom into practice and when they do so, they become that Way, for its factors become an integral part of their life. It was to humanity that the Buddha gave most of his important Teachings knowing that they could understand them, practise them and so come to realize them, (as the three sections of this book try to show).

A person may decide to devote life to selfish, unwholesome ends, a mere existence, or to give purpose to life by the practice of wholesome deeds which will make both self and others happy. It is true that there is a backlog of habit-tendencies from the past to influence such a person. Still, in many cases, one can make the vital decision to shape one's life in this way or that. In doing so, one also give shape to future existence, for as explained, wholesome deeds increase the power of good in the mind thus ensuring a happy rebirth; unwholesome deeds will only be productive, through the strengthening of a warped and diseased mind, of miserable future existences.

It is humans who can experience, if they wish, Enlightenment and become as the Buddha and the Arahants—this is the greatest blessing, for not only the secure tranquillity of one person's salvation is gained but out of Compassion the Path is shown to many others. Readers should understand that to be born human is especially precious, a great opportunity not to be wasted. In a Pali scripture the Buddha illustrated how rare it is to gain a human life once one has sunk into the three woeful states, with this simile: supposing a piece of wood with a hole in it drifted about in the ocean. In that ocean lived a one-eyed turtle which had to surface once in a hundred year to breathe. Even in one Great Aeon it would be most unlikely in surfacing, to put its head into the hole in that piece of wood. This is the sort of chance that beings in the states of deprivation have for gaining a human birth. The unhappy states are warnings to us that if we cultivate Greed, Aversion and Delusion in our minds, these types of birth will be the possible objects of our craving when we die.

Hungry Ghosts. * Below humanity in the spiritual scale come the hungry ghosts. These beings are sometimes seen, heard or otherwise experienced by some people. How do they come to that state? It is brought about by greed. Think of people whose attachments to money, material possessions, to family are very strong. The misers of this world, those who are the family octopi, those who rejoice in having more, better and bigger things than their nextdoor neighbours—such people are developing factors mind which if they persist in them will lead them to arise among the hungry ghosts.

"Hungry" means experiencing constantly unsatisfied cravings for contact with their former family whom in some cases they can alarm but not communicate with, or for their money and goods which they may actually see but cannot possess. They are in fact, in the position of Tantalus of Greek mythology, bound for a long time to crave what cannot be got. Life among them is long and miserable and many perceive neither night nor day, only an interminable greyness out of which blurred objects occasionally appear. When, owing to the exhaustion of the evil kamma which drove them into ghostly existence, they are reborn, it sometimes happens that if their birth is among men, they will be deformed in some say. However, investigation of various rebirth cases reveals that many whose lives were suddenly cut off, perhaps even most humans, spend a sort of intermediate existence in ghostly form in more or less comfortable circumstances while waiting for the chance to gain human rebirth consonant with their kamma.

The Pali simile describes the hungry ghost's state as that of a person who although weary can only find a broken-down tree giving patchy shade with rough, stony ground underneath it on which to take 'rest'. S/he experiences, as a hungry ghost, feelings which are **abundantly painful** and only slightly coloured with happiness.

Animals.* 'Downwards' again comes the animal kingdom, where delusion or dullness, the inability to understand, reigns supreme.

People who descend to a level lower than human by filling their mind to the exclusion of much else, with thoughts of food, drink and sex invite rebirth for themselves among animals.

Not only do animals lack the ability to understand but also their lives are for the most part quite miserable. Wild animals either live in fear of being killed by other animals or by meat-eating humanity, or if carnivorous themselves they are driven on by urges to kill others. All of them fear starvation about which they can do almost nothing. Domesticated animals suffer, many of them, in being used for our purposes. We crave their flesh, skin, furs, feathers, bones, oil or tusks; or we shoot them 'for fun' or hunt them in various ways to amuse ourselves (but does it amuse the hunted?). They must also bear the brunt of heat and cold, of parasites and diseases without being able to do anything effective to cure these ills. Fortunately for animals, their lives are usually short and their sufferings soon over. Although this is a blessing for them, it is difficult for a being experiencing animal life to get a chance to do something meritorious or even to understand the advantages of doing so, thus preventing the attainment of human birth until some result of good action from the distant past arises and gives freedom from continued becoming in the animal state. Born from the animal to human condition, they are often stupid, a hangover from their previous life.[12]

12. Theosophical teachings usually state that man can only progress from life to life, ever spiritually evolving to higher states. This is not accepted in Dhamma which takes note of the fact that men do not only progress, they also regress. No progress is to be seen in men who (to take extreme cases as more easily understandable) were S.S. Guards at Auschwitz or Belsen, or in those who planned and actually committed the dropping of the Atom Bombs in Japan, or those whose work is continually to butcher animals to satisfy human craving or in hardened criminals or the permanent inmates of mental hospitals and so on. All such are sliding down from human level to these subhuman states.

In Pali the simile speaks of a person going along and coming eventually to a cess-pit full of stinking filth—into which s/he falls and experiences, as animal, feelings, which are **painful, sharp, severe**.

As animals are within the field of human perception and it is known that they too have feelings of pleasure and pain so Buddhists generally treat them well. Buddhists do not agree that they are just made to be used anyhow by man.

Hells.* The lowest and most miserable condition of existence is not however within normal human experience: hell is not usually directly perceived by people. It seems that some with acute mental derangement really live in this life in hell, for their world is certainly not as ours. Also, the occasional meditator who either takes a wrong turn (very dangerous for sanity), or who is able to control the mind very well indeed, may also experience the hell-states. The hell-states comprise such extreme and violent experiences, such as intense heat and cold, unutterable filth, as well as demonic apparitions (all such phenomena being produced by the force of past unwholesome deeds in the minds of those who experience them).

According to Buddhist psychology, the mental factor of aversion is always linked to the experience of pain. One may be greedy and happy but never angry and happy at the same time. Anyone who cultures hatred, anger, malice, nurses revenge or keeps alive a grudge is bound to experience much suffering for s/he has laid hold of a very potent source of it. Those who exercise their hatred on others as in killing, torturing or maiming may expect birth in a state, compared in the scriptural simile to a pitful of glowing embers, where they will experience feelings which are **exclusively painful, sharp, severe**. Only in such an environment will they be able to experience all the misery which they, by their own cruelty to others, have brought upon themselves.

Life in the various hells is accordingly long, pointing out to us the gravity of the evil committed when, with a mind hate-filled, we bring sorrows upon others. To do so, is to invite continual torment and when out of this state finally, miserable and terrified beings eventually escape, laying hold of the result of some slightly wholesome action, they may ascend to animal birth. It is rare for a being to be able to jump from the hells to human condition. If this can be done, the human being resulting will often be both deformed and an idiot, a terrible reminder of the former existence. Visitors to Buddhist countries may sometimes notice such a person being helped by a relative to give alms or do some other act of merit in order that the deranged one may become whole in the next existence.

It will be noted of the different levels of existence described here that in every case they are experienced by sentient beings because of the cultivation of factors either wholesome or unwholesome. It is therefore true to say that when certain mental factors are present and produce in combination the arising of a certain type of mind, this will be productive of a corresponding environment. The Buddhist teachings on the existence of certain conditions for rebirth are therefore no empty fancy but stress the fact, everywhere taught in the Buddha's Teachings, of the paramount importance of the state of mind. According to the mind so is the world which is perceived, another illustration of Dependent Origination.

The mind, overcoming its mundane limitations, is able to attain the supermundane which lies 'beyond' all the various levels of existence (see III). An end of continued rebirth is only found when one arrives unshakably at the same insights which the Buddha and many others have known. Stopping the wheel of birth-and-death coincides with the knowledge of Perfection which the Buddha knew, the Great Peace of Nibbana. The Pali simile is exceptionally beautiful when describing Nibbana and is quoted here in full: "By encompassing mind with mind I understand a certain person thus: 'This person so behaves, has such deportment, the path taken is such that, by realizing for himself by direct knowledge here and now he enters upon and abides in the heart's deliverance and deliverance by wisdom that are taint-free, with exhaustion of taints.'

And then later on I see that he does that and is experiencing feelings that are **exclusively tranquil**. Suppose there were a lotus pond with clear, sweet and cool water, limpid, with smooth and delightful banks, while close to it lies a well-shaded forest thicket. Then a person might come along overcome and overpowered by the hot-weather heat, exhausted, parched and thirsty, heading directly by the only way for that very pool. One with vision having seen him, might say: 'As that good person so behaves, his deportment is such, the path that he has taken is such, that he will come to that lotus-pool. Later on he sees that he has gone down into the pond, has bathed in it and drunk of it, and having allayed all distress, exhaustion and fever, has got out again and is sitting or lying down in that forest thicket experiencing feelings that are **exclusively tranquil**." (Middle Collection, Discourse 12).

As Buddhism is a religion of Compassion as well of Wisdom, Buddhists give thought to and try to relieve the sufferings of those born in unfortunate states. Principally, this is done by performing wholesome actions and then devoting the merit accrued to the welfare of other beings. The teachings on the dedication of merit are another example of the skilful use of a doctrine as a 'means'. So that people do not try to hoard merit as 'their own' and so that they develop a sympathy with and wish to alleviate the sufferings of others, they are encouraged to devote merits to the unhappy beings. Very often, it is directed towards the hungry ghosts, and to past relations who may now be experiencing the woes of that realm; this has also the very practical benefit of appeasing such beings and ensuring that they do not trouble humanity.

Finally, it is necessary to answer one question which is, perhaps naively, quite often asked about rebirth: Now that the population of the world is increasing, where do all the 'new' people come from? This is largely answered above where it has been shown that the life of humanity is not isolated from other states of existence as individuals may spiritually evolve to other states or degenerate to the sub-human. The beings, both in the super- and in sub-human states, vastly outnumber the small race of mankind on this earth. (Think of the number of ants alone in Thailand compared with the human population!) But Buddhist thought is not limited to this insignificant planet and has always conceived of infinite numbers of vast world-systems (galaxies in modern parlance), inhabited in accordance with their conditions. The beings of one world-system are not isolated from those of another and although rebirth will usually take place in the same one, this is not necessarily the case. Usually however, a being human in the last birth and seeking human rebirth, will come to be born again amongst people of a similar group. Sometimes birth will take place even into the same family especially where family ties are strong. Religion, governing as it does many social matters and thus colouring a great deal of the environment, will for this reason frequently remain the same from birth to birth though this is by no means always so. Sex may also change.

IN THE BEGINNING

Having written in outline upon the why and wherefore of rebirth, one question at least remains unanswered: How and where did it all begin?

Of course, there must have been a beginning—or is this really necessary? If I consider that at one time I was not, then what has brought into existence this being now known by such-and-such a name? The usual religious answer is that a god or impersonal power created the universe, this planet and the beings on it. When we consider this, a further question inevitably arises: Where has this god or other power come from? If the reply is that s/he is eternal then why did s/he decide at some point in time to bring all this into existence? What for? His (or her) pleasure? Our tribulation? If a positive answer is given in either way, s/he can hardly be called Compassionate. An answer to all such enquiries which kills further investigation of the subject, is that the ways of god are inscrutable.

It is interesting how people often relegate god to the distant past of Creation or to the distant future of the judgement. This means that s/he has little relevance to their present life. S/He is perhaps a belief and s/he may be a craving (for a father, a mother, for eternal life, etc.) but when it comes to the living of everyday life then the god-idea rarely come to mind. This gives us a clue to one Buddhist attitude to the god-idea which is, even if s/he does exist what practical difference does it make to one's life here and now? Is not the distant past, like the distant future, strictly irrelevant to us at the present time? It is always the present which is important in the Dhamma, neither the past, often compared to a dream, nor the future which is likened to a mirage. What I do **now**, how I react **now**, these things are infinitely more relevant than speculations over distant events. These are said by the Buddha to be the tangle of Wrong Views, 'wrong' since no firm conclusions can be reached on the bases on which they are reared. What are these? Blind faith is one and craving is another. Moreover a hornet's nest is stirred up whenever opposing sets of 'beliefs' come into conflict and so-called 'religious' wars and persecutions are a pointer to how strong the attachment can be to Wrong Views. Why be tangled up in them?

The Buddha has said when answering a question on the length of an aeon*: "No beginning can be seen to beings, blinded by unknowing and driven on by craving who are hurrying through the round of birth-and-death." Thus for Buddhists, "in the beginning" has no meaning and no point in time can be found when there was a Creation; nor any Creator (we are all Creators and through our intentional action (kamma) bring about a continuous Creation).[13] It is not more puzzling to understand an

13. In Buddhism, unknowing or ignorance is described as the Creator, one which is in the heart of every unenlightened person and brings about the making of kamma and the various experiences of dukkha. Other aspects of 'god' are distributed under different aspects of Buddhism: judgement and retribution under kamma; eternality and unchangingness under Dhamma; as a being with powers over the world, one of the Brahma-gods, and so on. 'God' is a very complex idea and people even in one religious

infinity of birth-and-death rooted in unknowing than it is to talk of a Creator who was never born. Indeed, the former has a great advantage over the latter since unknowing is in one's own heart and may be removed by the appropriate training.

Events are dependent for their arising upon complex sets of conditions. Thus do all dhammas (events, things both mental and physical) come into existence and thus do they pass away. No beginning, no Maker need be sought, An ancient verse says:

> No god, no Brahma can be called
> The Maker of this Wheel of Life:
> Just empty phenomena roll on
> Dependent on conditions all.
>
> Path of Purification XIX; translated by Ven. Nyanamoli Thera

The Buddha spoke not only of innumerable systems of worlds grouped into what we should call galaxies,* but also of equally vast conceptions of time. The most ancient Buddhist texts speak of the various phases in the evolution and devolution over enormous time-periods of these galaxies; how they are gradually formed and how after a period of relative stability during which life may be found on their worlds, how, inevitably having come into existence, they must in due course decline and destruct. All this is the working of processes, one event leading quite naturally to another. While watches do have watch-makers, they need also an infinity of other factors; in the same way the universe unrolls and rolls up by the forces that inhere in it.

What exactly did the Buddha have to say about god? Did he maintain silence on this topic, a statement one sees printed so many times? The account given by him on the genesis of the 'Creator' will be enough to settle this question: It happens that at the

---

tradition, have their own ideas as to what constitutes 'god.' In Buddhist tradition there is no one concept which cover this mixture of ideas.

beginning of a new cycle (after one of the periodic cosmic destructions), a being according to his kamma is born into a heavenly state where no other beings are to be found (his kamma being a condition for the arising of that particular heavenly experience).[14] He does not remember his past life among the gods in the 'higher' heavens and comes to believe during the passing of ages that he has lived there **forever**. When immense spans of time have passed, he wishes for the company of others and then, since according to their kamma some other beings appear in that realm, he comes to believe that they were produced by his will. From this he goes on to glorify himself, his supposed 'creation' aiding his vanity since they do not remember their past lives and so imagine that they are the creatures of Brahma. One of these great Brahmas by the name of Baka, was made to see the hollowness of his claims to eternal existence and creatorhood when the Buddha in meditation (remember that these realms exist in the dimension of mind) paid a visit to that realm.

The Buddhist attitude to God or Brahma the Creator is fairly summed up in these verses:

> *If He indeed has lordship in the world,*
> *God, Lord of beings all and humankind,*
> *Why in the world has He arranged travail?*
> *And why for all there's not just happiness?*
> *If He indeed has Lordship in the world,*
> *God, Lord of beings all and humankind,*
> *What purpose has He made a world of lies*

---

14. Since these matters are all contained in the discourses of the Buddha, it makes no sense to talk of him as an 'agnostic' (one who does not know). On the contrary, he should be called a gnostic or One-who-knows (janata). He is also called Sabbannu, the 'All-knower.' 'All-knowing' means that to whatever subject the Buddha turned his attention, all the contents of that were known to him. It does not mean that he always knew everything about every subject all at once—a claim he specifically denied about himself.

with fraud and faults, with what's unjust [15] *as well?*
If He indeed has Lordship in the world,
God, Lord of beings all and humankind,
Unrighteous is that Lord of beings then
Who wrong arranged and not the Dhamma true.

Bhuridatta Jataka, No. 453, verses 154–56

The greater the power of God then the less will be the ability of humanity to do what is wholesome or unwholesome (this means predistinarian doctrines). These were the provocation for the following lines:

If God directs the lives of all that live,
Kammas good and evil, fortune, ruin too,
Then humans are but servants of his will,
While God is stained by what he's done as well.

Mahabodhi Jataka, No. 528, verse 19

THE WORLD

From what has been written above the reader will now understand that 'world'* in the Buddhist teachings has a great range and does not only refer to what we perceive with the senses at the present time. It is kept in existence by beings who have craving to be born in various ways according to their kamma. All the three spheres— Sensuality, Subtle Form and Formlessness—are filled with beings arising and passing away, all of them bound to the wheel of repeated birth and death. This wandering on and on through the various spheres, lodging for a while on this or that plane, is called Samsara. Literally, this is the 'Wandering-on' in birth and death.

---

15. In these verses the words 'unjust,' 'unrighteous,' and 'wrong' all translate the literal 'what is not Dhamma'. 'Dhamma true' in the last line is really 'the Dhamma that IS.'

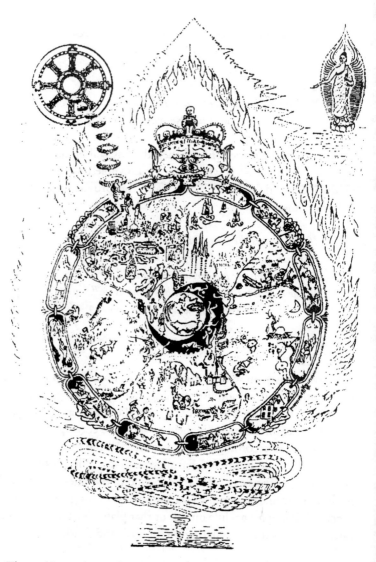

The teaching-aid more than 2,000 years old, showing the world of wondering-on in birth and death, formerly painted in the gateways of Buddhist monasteries in India.

One should not have the idea that the world we know here has some glorious and predetermined destiny towards which events are moving. Events are determined by the kammas made by individual people and the whole fabric of 'our' world is conditioned and goes according to the minds of human beings. If these deteriorate, becoming further infected with Greed, Aversion and Delusion, then this world is bound to decline.

At present, there is no doubt that human beings are very clever at controlling exterior factors in the world due to our scientific progress, but we may doubt if we are advancing very fast in the direction of purity of heart. In fact, capitalism and advertising stimulate more Greed and Delusion while communism and nuclear armaments make possible more terrible expressions of Aversion. Advance can be seen in suppression by modern treatments of physical diseases but decline is shown by the great increase in mental diseases, addiction to drink and drugs, juvenile delinquency, lowering moral standards and violence generally.

The world has always been like this: some factors advancing, some declining, for this state of things is never stable. Those who work in the world can at best, keep it patched up and try to prevent deterioration. Before going on to say how this can be done, the accompanying diagram showing "The Wheel of Life" should be explained briefly.

In the centre, Greed (a cock), Aversion (a snake) and Delusion (a pig) are depicted as the root-causes for existence. Outside this centre are the white and the black paths. On the former, people are walking uprightly in the beneficial way of practice, while in the latter naked humans (symbolizing shamelessness) fall downwards by their evil deeds. From the white path the two happy births may be entered but those upon the black path fall into the three unhappy conditions. The happy births are shown at the top—the gods to the right (with the quarrelsome titans just below), and humanity to the left. The world of hungry ghosts is lower right, animals are lower left and at the bottom of the circle there are the hells. Surrounding these five (or six) conditions there are the twelve links of Dependent Arising beginning with unknowing—the blind old woman leaning on a stick, and concluded by old age and death. This intricate aspect of conditionality cannot be explained in the limited space here (but see Supermundane Wisdom and its Perfection). All of our life is summed up in these twelve links. These links and the worlds contained by them are gripped by the Demon Impermanence; they are all devoured by him. On his head he wears the crown of five skulls symbolizing the five unstable and dangerous groups comprising our personality. The whole wheel is ringed about by flames, the searing heat of Greed, Aversion and Delusion. Below the wheel a tail without beginning is the tale of our own births and deaths without beginning; while to the upper left the Dhamma-path well-expounded by the Buddha leads from his mouth to the Dhamma-wheel, a symbol of Nibbana. And to the right above stands the Buddha upon the further shore of Nibbana, he who has safely crossed the ocean of painful wandering-on, and warns us who are still running up and down on this bank, of the dangers which face us everywhere. This picture can be explained in great detail but this brief summary must suffice here. As a 'teaching aid' for Dhamma it was possibly designed by the Buddha himself but certainly the text in which it is described is not less than two thousand years old. It incorporates all the important Dhamma-teachings and points the way to happiness for humanity and all beings.

Now, what can be done about the world when it is in this state: The Buddha, when asked about the world, once replied that 'world' means: "the eye and sights, the ear and sounds, the nose and smells, the tongue and tastes, the body and touches, the mind and thoughts." He said that no world could be explained by anyone apart from this world, for all of our experience, all of our knowledge is contained in these twelve categories. Collectively, they are called 'the All.' 'To do something about the world' therefore means primarily to do something about oneself. When one's own world, or personality improves by the practice of Dhamma, other people are benefited automatically. "Protecting oneself, one protects others" these are the Buddha's words. It is certain that one can protect and improve oneself by elimination of Greed, Aversion and Delusion, but if one starts work on others there is no certainty of success. One who practises Dhamma should get to work where success is assured—in oneself.

THREE ROOTS OF EVIL

As we have seen, with crooked or unwholesome states of mind present, one experiences sufferings; with their refinement and with the development of wholesome states, one may know the spiritual joys of heaven; finally, having liberated oneself with the sword of Wisdom from even a desire for the wholesome, one comes to know the ineffable—Nibbana. Is one afflicted with the wandering-on in birth-and-death? Or does one exhibit in every action, supremely perfect Purity, Wisdom and Compassion as an Enlightened being? In one case the mind[16] has not been cultured at all, while in the other it has attained such an incomparably vast change in function that although one may speak of the Enlightened person as possessed of such-and-such mental powers, such a condition is really beyond all classification.

In the Dhamma there exist a number of different classifications of 'mental' states* having various mental factors.* The purpose of these teachings is to enable psychological analysis to be made so that unwholesome states are quickly detected and broken up, wholesome states vigorously promoted and both Collectedness and Wisdom aided.[17] The actual working of this pragmatic psychology

16. The English word 'mind' does not fit very well the Pali: citta. All mental and emotional processes are included in the latter which comprises the four mental groups: Feeling, Memory/Recognition, Mental Formations and Consciousness. This should be remembered when speaking of 'mind' in a Buddhist context.

17. There is some need to stress also that Buddhism has no 'philosophy' which is divorced from either its practice or its realization. Such philosophy lacking a secure basis in Virtue, Collectedness and Wisdom and representing some philosophers' present views, is really no philosophy at all, only a species of speculation.

cannot be dealt with here and all that can be said is that it is an attempt to formulate in useful concepts dynamic mental states as opposed to static ideas such as 'mind,' 'soul,' etc.

The experiences which most people regard as 'normal' knowledge are actually all twisted to a greater or lesser extent by the sense of 'I' and the sense of what is outside 'I.' Where this distinction is made, there is dualism and in its wake comes Greed (what 'I' want and like), Aversion (what 'I' dislike or do not want) and Delusion (the basic unknowing that anything is wrong involving attitudes of 'I do not know' and 'I do not want to know'). This twisting gives rise not to perception of the world as it really is, but to an 'I-possessed' world, that is, one coloured by all the characteristic patterns of thought and memories which, when one links the past to the present and that in turn to expectations of the future, constitute one's own mental image of oneself. It is the latter which gets in the way of clear-seeing or Insight, for we are perpetually seeing the world through 'I-coloured' spectacles. It seems more or less to revolve about oneself, that is, all the perceived events by way of the various senses (including mind-sense) are in some way automatically related to the 'I'. Either they are thought of as part of the 'I', as belonging to it, as experienced by it, as wished for by it, as detested by it, as different to it—or, the negative relations as, 'not-I' etc. The 'I-mine' which brings about selfishness or egocentricity, is the source of all our suffering for it brings in its wake, desire for, dislike of and dull indifference to—all emotional attitudes which will guarantee that true lasting happiness is not found.

Greed may be associated with temporary pleasure, but once the object of one's desire is got at, desire ceases and the pleasure which one derives from it is always more or less fleeting as the object is, in any case, impermanent.

Aversion in all its graded tones is the most effective way to destroy happiness and bring about misery. Whether it is self-hatred or dislike of others, both produce much suffering, nor will dislike of objects or circumstances help one to happiness. A person who constantly develops anger, alienates himself from the rest of humanity (indeed from all other creatures), goes sour inside and is storing up very unpleasant kamma which will result in great unhappiness to be experienced in the future.

Dullness or Delusion just prevents one seeing what really leads to happiness and what to unhappiness. Even if the whole of the Buddha's Way to Perfection, well explained and clear as a detailed map, were laid out in front of a person suffering particularly from this disease, it would not be understood.

Although it is not a very welcome conclusion, 'I' get born into this round of birth and death because of the Three Roots of Evil.* The sense of 'I' is founded upon Greed, Aversion and Delusion, a nasty knock for the ego! And the 'I-sense' vanishes when the Three Roots are eradicated.

From these three, Greed, Aversion and Delusion, singly or in combination, all the various unwholesome states spring. They are also called Diseases, and according to Buddhist psychology anyone who permits them to spring up and flourish in his mind, is mentally diseased. Lunatics, far from all being safely restrained in hospitals, are in fact everywhere; we only keep in custody the most extreme examples in whom these Roots range unchecked, choking all wholesome consciousness. All those who have not known Supreme Wisdom are to some degree mentally deranged, their consciousness split and warped. The only mentally 'whole' ones are those who have known the Whole or 'the All' thoroughly and are, therefore, also 'holy' in the true sense of this much misused word. (It is noteworthy that 'whole' and 'holy' are etymologically related).

THE INVERSIONS

From these Unwholesome Roots arise the more complex Inversions,* that is to say when we regard people, objects and even notions, all of which are ever-changing from moment to moment, as permanent; what is really fraught with unsatisfactoriness as being pleasant; all phenomena, both form and mentality, the living and the inanimate, all of which really do not possess any essence, soul or self, as in fact being in possession of some such underlying entity; and lastly, the inversion which regards what is really unlovely, subject to decay and even 'messy', as being beautiful.

These Inversions exist in three degrees of intensity, and are respectively called the Inversion of Perception, that of Mind and that of Views. The first means that only one's perception is distorted and one mistakenly perceives things as they are not (as seeing a rope but mistaking it for a snake, or hearing wind wail and mistaking it for ghosts, etc). Inversion of Mind is the regarding of thoughts which are actually demeritorious and will lead to unhappiness as leading to happiness (as the dwelling in anticipation on some future object of pleasure, a person, place or thing which the inverted mind regards as giving real happiness). This may be merely an intellectual misunderstanding and the result of false information or training but the third degree of intensity which is most serious involves an inverted emotional attitude. This is the Inversion of Views as when some political, philosophical or religious view is seized on and regarded as being ultimate truth, (as in faith-religions where wisdom is relegated to the background, or in philosophies not securely based on Insight but merely on speculation, or in the special class of the latter, the materialistic and dogmatic pseudo-religions of the present, such as Communism or Fascism) without having subjected it to the searching test of Insight-Wisdom by way of meditation which alone reveals underlying Truth.

Each of the four above mentioned Inversions may be experienced in these three intensities and the following will clarify the meaning of the former. In the first, we are deceived by the momentary exterior appearances of things. They do not appear to be changing; they appear to our Delusion-dulled senses as static. We do not perceive processes in dynamic change but only as we think, entities which go on existing. Similarity, due to a line of change in a given direction, is often mistaken for sameness. If this misapprehension is firmly rooted in our minds, all sorts of attachments and cravings for people and things (including attachment to oneself) will be formed and these bring with them much sorrow, for to regard people and things in this way is to regard them as through a distorting glass. It is not seeing them correctly, it is seeing them invertedly as though permanent.

Second, the unsatisfactory dukkha invertedly appears to be pleasant. Thus people fritter away much of their precious lives on this or that 'pleasure' and as they never actually get the satisfaction they crave for, so they are driven on from one thing to another. 'Pleasures' may produce temporary feelings of ease, of worldly happiness, but they are always linked to succeeding disappointment, regret, longing for some other emotion indicating an absence of real satisfaction. Those who actually rejoice in Greed, Aversion or Delusion are of course, invertedly trying to enjoy what is not enjoyable. Dukkha is linked to any mental state into which the above Three Roots enter. Nothing really satisfactory can be expected where they operate as they certainly do in turning round what is by nature unsatisfactory and making it appear the opposite.

The third mode of these Inversions in which objects are regarded as having a permanent essence, or people a self or soul, is the outcome of not perceiving the first and second above. In, or behind, everchanging processes there cannot be anything unchanging for, first, how could the impermanent be related to something which would be its opposite? Second, such permanence is unknown both to the world investigated through Insight-meditation and also to all the array of modern sciences. Even in the realms of nuclear physics, no essences unchanging have been found—all is in flux, in continuous change.

Again, the really permanent would also be a source of lasting satisfaction but as we have seen, such satisfaction is not to be obtained from the usual search among things, places and people so that it is true to say that dissatisfaction (dukkha) arises from the transitory. As things, etc., are not perceived as changing, we not only invertedly think that they do not change (and are disappointed when they shatter our expectations) but also conclude from the projection of our own

'I-sense' on to such people and things, that they have an inward permanence, an undying essence or noumena. Because most people do not possess the faculty of Insight which penetrates beyond appearances and reveals the world as it really is, so it is not commonly realized that objects—a Rolls Royce, or a daisy, or Mr. Jones, or a mosquito, or me, or this earth, or the universe—are not unitary 'things' all-of-a-lump but are composed in reality of hosts of conditions related together. A moment or two's thought about this may dispose readers to agree. The trouble is that intellectual agreement with regard to the inversions and especially this one, is certainly not enough.

Lastly, the unlovely is seen as beautiful. Not aware of the changeful nature of things, not seeing that beauty now will tomorrow be withered, persons and things are seized on as really beautiful. This body, for instance may, while it is young and unwrinkled, appear pleasant to look at but one does not, regarding it in this way, note two important facts: first, that it is inevitably progressing to decay, disease, old age and finally death, in which states it is seldom thought beautiful—but this we forget due to this inversion; and second, it is even now composed of bits and pieces which we may know are there, but which we have not seen (for instance, our own lungs or entrails), and which certainly most people would not like to see. The skin hides much, which if it were laid out on a table in front of us, would very probably make us sick. And yet this is our beautiful body and it is the same with the other beautiful bodies to which we are attached. The skin is only a fraction of an inch thick, yet just by removing this alone the beautiful girl or the handsome man are revealed as bloody messes. Who could have desire for them? This is a good example of the unlovely regarded as being lovely.

THREE MARKS OF EXISTENCE

When the first three modes of the Inversions no longer mislead one, three related insights are obtained into the nature of oneself and hence of all reality: one sees that all conditioned 'things' in oneself or exterior, sentient or non-sentient, are **Impermanent**,* that while one craves, all conditioned 'things' are **Unsatisfactory (dukkha)** and that no owner is found within oneself—that all events are **Insubstantial** or **No-self.***

These are called the Three Marks of Existence* and should be examined a little more fully as the insight meditations called Clear Seeing* are aimed at uncovering them. It is not possible to discern them however, without first calming the agitated mind. All of these insights must be obtained in one's continuity of mind and body, if they are to be effective in destroying the mental stains such as the Three Roots, etc. We are merely examining them intellectually.

Regarding the first one, though we may see leaves on a tree, some young and unfolding, some mature, while others are sere and yellow, impermanence does not strike home in our hearts. Although our hair changes from black, to grey, to white over the years, we do not realize what is so obviously being preached by this change—impermanence. There is a vast difference between occasionally acquiescing in the mind and admitting with the tongue the truth of Impermanence, and actually realizing it constantly in the heart. The trouble is that while intellectually we may accept impermanence as valid truth, emotionally we do not admit it, specially in regard to 'I' and 'mine.' But whatever our unwholesome emotions of Greed, etc., may or may not admit, impermanence remains a truth, and the sooner we come to realize through Insight that it is a truth, the happier we shall be, because our mode of thought will thus be nearer to reality.

Second, it is easy to say, 'Oh yes, unsatisfactory conditions (dukkha) are produced by craving.' But it is not enough to leave it at that. That craving has really to be rooted out of one's mental states, again by Insight, so that dukkha ceases to affect one. This is only a Truth when one sees with Wisdom that it is so. Until that time, it remains a teaching, albeit a good one, from which much sound guidance may be obtained for the conduct of life.

The last is most difficult to understand. The former two may be mentally accepted after certain data from sense-experience has been examined but the Mark of No-self cannot be penetrated so easily. It has in fact, to be realized after prolonged meditation and will be known when the other related Marks are fully realized. It is also the most emotionally disturbing of these Marks since it runs directly counter to the ordinary egocentric notions, which without thinking and ruled by the third mode of Inversion, people usually suppose to be true. If one examines a chair, most people (except a few philosophers holding to the speculations of the Greeks), will agree that the chair cannot be found apart from it parts. Take it to pieces and one is left with legs, back seat, cushions and so on—but 'chair' has disappeared. By chopping all these parts into little pieces, neither 'chair' nor 'leg', 'back', etc., can be found—only pieces of wood. Going further, no chair at all can be perceived after all these pieces of wood have been burnt and only ashes remain, and so on, for such processes are without end. When one examines things in this light, only processes are to be found, no actual, abiding substantial 'things'. Now, this is all very well applied to a chair but not all acceptable to many people if it is applied to one's precious 'self'. Break it up, what does one find? The Buddha in one classification, enumerated Five Groups: a body; feeling, (pleasant, painful and neither); recognition/memory (or things perceived through the senses); thoughts; and consciousness (by way of eye, ear, nose, tongue, body and mind). Now where is this owner, 'myself'? The self, from this illustration, is seen to be compounded of different factors and while it does exist relatively, our great mistake is to suppose that it exists as a 'thing', as a whole, or that there is some 'owner' who really is my 'self'. At every stage of analysis, which for the uprooting the Inversions must proceed with one's 'own' mind-body and not be exercised upon chairs, it is found that whatever are the parts with which one is dealing, they are all without an owner, even down to the most minute particles or to the most fleeting of events, they will be seen by intense Insight, to be void of self, to be not-self. We shall, in Part III, consider Not-self and Voidness again.

MERITS AND PERFECTIONS

Before discussing Buddhist practice, which begins in a very down-to-earth way and is not at all 'up in the air', we must descend from these heights to examine its beginnings.

These are found in what is called 'merit-making' (a rather poor translation), and the idea of merit* should be briefly examined here. Merit is derived from the performance of all wholesome actions whether they are mental, verbal or involve the body for their principle expression. Merit is defined by saying that **it cleanses and purifies the mind of the doer.** That is the doing of wholesome kamma increases the strength of the Roots of Wholesomeness while decreasing the hold of the Unwholesome Roots. Because of the increase of what is wholesome and the weakening of the unwholesome, it is said that merit opens doors and makes opportunities. It increases one's chances of, for instance, a good education, possessing or obtaining wealth, hearing the Dhamma, taking an interest in it, and training oneself therein. It is worth remembering that merit opens doors. Hence we talk about the stock of merit or the roots of merit which a person has acquired.

How has it been acquired? By such actions as those listed in the Ten Ways of Making Merit: Giving, Virtue, Collectedness (or meditation), Reverence, Helpfulness, Dedication of Merits to others, Rejoicing in other' Merits, Listening to Dhamma, Pointing-out (teaching) the Dhamma, (and as a result) Straightening-out one's views. There is no room here to expand on these ten aspects of merit-making though many of them are explained elsewhere in this book, but they are very important to all Buddhists. While some of them are taken for granted in the East where they are frequently practised, they are all of great importance for Buddhists in the 'West'. One may find there many a Buddhist who has by reading books and attending lectures acquired sufficient learning to explain such difficult ideas as Nibbana or Not-self but while in theory the topmost heights of Buddhist Teaching can be explained, the lives of some of these people may be full of conflicts internal and external. The gap between the intellectual and the practical then becomes painfully obvious if not to oneself, then certainly it will be so to others. These ten ways of merit-making fell one how to fill one's days with the most perfitable actions, since meritorious actions help to heal the rift between intellect and emotions.

The motive which moves a person to make merit is happiness here and now and future happiness in a world beyond.[18] This is the realistic attitude for while one has selfishness and an apparent 'self', truly altruistic actions are impossible. The practice of Dhamma always benefits other beings. Popular merit-making, as practised in Thailand, is often a communal activity involving all the village or else a party of friends, or a family, and others though they may bring nothing are very welcome to join in. Bells and drums and joyful shouting in procession inform others of merit-making so that they may either join, or else be happy that others are happy. And this is in itself merit. We should remember that although other forms of merit-making are not communal, such as observing the precepts, practising meditation or straightening-out one's views, they are still for others' good.

While merit is the practical outcome of increasing the strength of the Wholesome Roots, it will not by itself cut off mental defilements or the Evil Roots. Wisdom is needed for this and in

18. It has been said, both in the Buddha's day and recently, that Buddhism is 'selfish'. If ever a charge was anomalous, it is this one! Before one can give spiritual help to others, self-help is essential. The Buddha said: "How can one person stuck in the mud pull out another also stuck in the mud?" Buddhists are convinced that saving others can only be effectively accomplished when one has gone at least some way towards saving oneself. The latter sentence shows the inadequacies of language for to save oneself in the Buddhist sense is completely to have uprooted even the slightest conceptions of self, to be utterly selfless, to be naturally devoted to the "welfare and happiness of gods and men."

the higher ranges of Buddhist practice we speak not of merit but of the Perfecting Qualities, or the Perfections.* Merit becomes a Perfection when it is performed completely without reference to the self-idea. When one is giving a gift, it is not 'I am giving' but just 'there is giving', for bare attention reveals just processes void of self. Similarly, there is no 'he is receiving' but just 'there is receiving', while the action itself has no substance either. This seeing-things-as-they-really-are goes beyond merit because it is beyond any idea of a self to whom that merit could belong. Merits take one to birth as humans or to heavenly realms but Perfections take one beyond birth, to the other Shore of Nibbana.

The Ten Perfections listed below are selected from both the Pali and Sanskrit lists, though many are common to both. They will be treated under the sections of practice to which they refer. These Perfections may of course, all be practised by those who, while they aspire to Enlightenment, have not yet entered on the path of Wisdom. In that case they will be just mundane Perfections or the practice of very good qualities.

THE PERFECTIONS OF

(see under)

Mundane Wisdom	RENUNCIATION ASPIRATION	(preliminaries)
Virtue	GIVING VIRTUE	(the basis)
Meditation	PATIENCE ENERGY COLLECTEDNESS	(additional qualities)
Supermundane Wisdom	WISDOM WHOLESOME MEANS TRUTH	(with all Perfections)

THE MIDDLE PATH OF PRACTICE*

Something should be said here of the Way whereby perfection may be reached. Often called the 'Middle Way', it is more accurately translated as the Middle Path of Practice. We should understand that when the Buddha teaches this Path as avoiding all extremes, that does not mean a sort of Anglo-Saxon compromise between everything! While compromise has its uses, it is not what is meant by a Middle Path avoiding extremes. In what respects then, is it the path which is Dhamma, 'in the middle'?

'Middle' here has such a great variety of applications that it is only possible to mention a few, but basically it may be defined as **the transcending of all extremes by the Way of Dhamma.** Let us consider a few applications of this principle when the meaning will become clear. In the Buddha's very first discourse, "The Turning of the Dhamma-Wheel", he speaks of two unwholesome and unworthy extremes for the conduct of these who have left their homes to take up a religious life. One is indulgence in pleasures of the sense that is, giving into the Evil Root of Greed, while the other is the mortification of the body (that is, succumbing to the Evil Root of Aversion—in this case, self-hatred). Further, he speak of the Middle Path of Practice which he has found as a result of Enlightenment following which one will gradually progress (quickly or slowly depending on the weakness or strength respectively, of the mental defilements such as Evil Roots) through Virtue, Collectedness, and Wisdom, thus overcoming and finally destroying these Roots altogether. Here we see the Middle Path at work transcending extremes in the sphere of conduct.

Let us take another aspect of the human character—the holding of views. Views, whether speculations, dogmatic assumptions or justification, are defined by Buddhist tradition as **incomplete knowledge seized upon, believed in and distorted by the interaction of the Evil Roots.** The endless wrangling of philosophers and theologians, and of political messiahs in our days, would be considerably abated if it was clearly understood WHY such-and-such beliefs were held. Followers seldom question, while the leaders who are left to do the thinking usually fail to realize their own cravings are in the background of the views they express. Craving is analysed into three sorts: craving for sensual pleasures, craving for being (existence) and craving for non- being or non-existence. It is plain to see that hedonic materialism is grounded on the first of these, while the eternalist religions of God, soul, everlasting life and so forth are rooted in the second craving. Out of the third spring the annihilationist systems such as the idealistic materialism of Communist dogma. While the first two are rooted in Greed, the third one has its roots in Aversion and all spring up from the taproot of Delusion. The Middle Path of Practice transcends all views because, when analyzed, they are all found to be one-sided obsessions rooted in some strong and often unseen emotion.

If we now examine the course of training, the Middle Path of Practice can be seen at work among these emotional obsessions. How do people react to an emotional upsurge of some kind? Generally, two courses are known to them, that is, they either indulge, or else suppress. By acting in either way they will only come to increase the dukkha from which they suffer. What then is the Middle Path of Practice? It is the Way of Mindfulness about which the succeeding section will have something to say and whereby instead of entangling oneself further in the wandering-on of birth-and-death, one finds the way out.

The Middle Path pervades a Buddhist's life leading one to practise what is wholesome and finally to transcend even the most subtle aspects of views when the evil roots are eradicated. Then the viewless Enlightenment will know the truth, according with what really is.

PART II

WHAT DO BUDDHISTS PRACTISE ?

Buddhists practise in order to realize what at first was accepted with faith. In this way faith is not divorced from practice. It would not be true to say that a Buddhist convinces himself of the truth of the Buddha's Teachings, since the course of practice prescribed includes the development of Wisdom which uproots mere beliefs and views while establishing one in the secure Refuge of Dhamma which is the perception of things as they really are.

THE GEM OF THE SANGHA (ORDER)

The last of the Three Refuges is still to be considered. It has been left over for this section as it is more appropriate to consider it under practice.

The Teachings of the Buddha are for everyone.[19] No one has been excluded from becoming a Buddhist by sex, race or colour. It

---

19. There is a strange idea current in some places, that Buddhism is only for monks. Nothing could be further from the truth. As we hope to show here, there is something for everyone to do, whether sangha or laity. It is true that many of the Buddha's discourses are addressed to monks but this does not preclude the use of their contents by the laity. How much of Buddhist Teaching one applies to one's life, does to a great extent depend on one's keenness and determination. Sangha are in surroundings more conducive to the application of the Buddha's Teachings as they should have less distractions than do the laity. Even among monks, ability and interest naturally vary, especially when there are 250,000 of

depends upon the individual Buddhist (and that person's circumstances) whether one remains in lay society or becomes a monk or nun. The benefit which each class derives from the other is mutual: the lay people give robes, food, shelter and medicines to the monks (and to a lesser extent to the nuns), and these are a monk's supports for his life. The giving of food is seen everywhere in Thailand between six and eight every morning[20] but robes, shelter and medicines are given on other occasions. The monks and nuns on their part, give something most precious to the laity: the Dhamma that they have studied, practised and realized. Thus lay Buddhists can easily find advice and help in a monastery from one of the teachers there or perhaps from a relative who is practising either permanently or for some time as monk or nun. And so, a balance is preserved, each group giving to the other something necessary for livelihood.

SOMETHING ABOUT ITS RULES

Monks and novices have sets of rules to guide them in their life and these, being voluntarily observed as ways of self-training, may be equally voluntarily relinquished, as when a monk becomes a novice again or reverts to the state of a layman. It is a common practice for

---

them as in Thailand. The word 'priest' should never be used for a bhikkhu, the best translation being 'monk.' It is true though that it is harder for a women to ordain and live as a Buddhist nun than it is for a man to get ordination as a monk.

20. Buddhist monks and nuns do not beg for their food nor are they beggars. A strict code of conduct regulates a monk's round to collect food. He may not for instance, make any noise cry out or sing—in order to attract people's attention. He walks silently and in the case of meditating monks, with a mind concentrated on his subject of meditation, and accepts whatever people like to give him. The Buddha once gravely accepted the offering of a poor girl who had nothing else to give except a chapatti: the girl had faith in the Great Teacher. From this one learns that it is not what is given that is important, but rather how a thing is given. The monk is to be content with whatever he is given, regarding the food as a medicine to keep the mind-body going on.

laymen to spend some time as a novice or monk, (the latter ordination is only given to persons over the age of 20 years). Usually this is done when school or college is finished, before taking up work, and for a period of three of four months from approximately July to October or November. This period, when monks must reside in one monastery is known in Thailand as 'Phansa' (or 'Vassa' in Pali), meaning 'The Rains,' originally just a time to be sheltered from the monsoon and now devoted to learning, the practice of meditation, in any case a time for intensified spiritual activity. After the Rains are over, monks are free to go to other monasteries or into the forest as they wish (unless they are still 'new' monks in the charge of their teacher). In the Buddhist Order, monks should not possess money and so observe 'poverty' in the sense of Christian monasticism.

As monks, they must of course, refrain from any sexual intercourse, thus observing 'chastity'. But they have not the rule to observe unquestioning 'obedience' though they have obligations as disciples of a teacher and all good monks honour these strictly. When, after at least five years, they have some learning and experience, knowing their rules well, they are free to wander here and there as they choose, seeking good teachers, or practising by themselves.

Mention should be made of the four most important precepts in the monk's code,* for breaking which he is expelled from the Order, never being able in this life to become a monk again. These four rules are: (1) Never to have any sexual relations, (2) Never deliberately to kill a human being, or to order persons to kill either other human beings or themselves, (3) Never to take anything (of some considerable value) that does not belong to one with the intention of possessing it oneself, (4) Never to claim falsely any spiritual attainment, power, or degree of Enlightenment (he is excused if he is mad, conceited or not serious).

A monk's actual possessions are very few and any other objects around him should be regarded by him as on loan from the Order.

He has only eight Requisites: An outer double-thick 'cloak', an upper-robe, an under-robe, a bowl to collect food, a needle and thread to repair his robes, a waistband for his under-robe, a razor, and a water-strainer to exclude small creatures from his drinking water so that neither they nor himself, are harmed.

As to his duties, they are simple but not easy to perform. He should endeavour to have wide learning and deep understanding of all that his Teacher the Enlightened One, has taught: he should practise the Teaching, observing Virtue, strengthening Collectedness and developing Wisdom; he will then realize the Buddha's Teachings according to his practice of them; and finally, depending upon his abilities, he may teach by his own example, by preaching, by writing books, etc.

REFUGE IN THE NOBLE COMMUNITY

When going for Refuge to the Sangha, one should not think of doing so to the whole body of monks for though a few of them are Noble,* the true nobility experienced after fire of Wisdom has burnt up the defilements,* the majority are still worldings. Among the laity too, there may be those who are Noble. The Noble monks, nuns and laity together form the Noble community which, as it is made up of those who are freeing and have freed themselves from bondage is truly a secure refuge. That lay-people may attain this supermundane Nobility should be sufficient to prove that this Teaching is meant also for them, though to attain they must practise thoroughly.

The Jewel of the Noble community has included many great Enlightened monks from the immediate disciples of the Buddha, such as the Venerables Anna-Kondanna, Sariputta, Moggallana, Mahakassapa, Ananda; and Venerable Nuns such as Mahapajapati, Khema, Uppalavanna, Dhammadinna, with laymen such as the benevolent Anathapindika and famous laywomen as was Visakha. This great procession of Enlightened disciples continues down the ages to the present day. Those who have done many meritorious deeds in the past could, if they searched with a sincere desire to learn, find a good teacher in Thailand today.

Although one may go for Refuge to the exterior Noble Order, one should seek for the real refuge within. This is the collection of Noble Qualities (such as the Powers of Faith, Energy, Mindfulness, Collectedness and Wisdom) which will lead one, balanced and correctly cultured, also to become a member of the Noble community.

In conclusion, it may be mentioned that in Thailand at the present time there are no fully-ordained Buddhist nuns, their line of ordination having died out in Sri Lanka over one thousand years ago. Another line of nun-ordination does however survive in China, Vietnam and Korea. Buddhist nuns in Thailand now are Eight-Precept laywomen, wearing white garments, shaving the head and devoting themselves to religious life. There are movements afoot to reinstate the Order of Nuns in the southern Buddhist countries but this will take time.

After describing Buddhist beliefs and their basis in the Triple Gem or Threefold Refuge, it is now time to outline what Buddhists practise in order to realize the Teachings of the Enlightened One and so substantiate within their own experience, the doctrines which initially they believed.

As a frame for the vast mass of teachings which would qualify to be considered here, an ancient threefold summary of the Teaching is used: Virtue, Collectedness and Wisdom. The Buddha has concisely formulated them in a verse famous them in a verse famous in all Buddhist lands:

> *Every evil never doing, (refers to Virtue)*
> *And in wholesomeness increasing, (to Collectedness)*
> *And one's heart well-purifying, (to Wisdom)*
> *This is the Buddhas' Teaching.*
>
> Dhammapada 183

These are known as the Three Trainings but since the last one, Wisdom, is both mundane and Supermundane, four sections have been devised as comprising the range (though far from the full substance) of the Dhamma: Mundane Wisdom, Virtue, Collectedness and Supermundane Wisdom.

1. MUNDANE WISDOM

This is quite naturally present when anyone begins to be interested in Buddhist Teachings. From reading, from conversations with Buddhists, from lectures, or in other ways, one comes to appreciate the Dhamma for such characteristics as its appeal to clear-thinking, fearlessness of free enquiry, tolerance, wide understanding of others' religions, helpfulness in daily life, practicability, and the gradual Way in which it proceeds, one factor leading on to the next—such points as these may impress even a casual inquirer. An earnest student will pursue such matters and find even greater delight in the ever-deepening vistas of the Buddhist Way.

In such ways, mundane wisdom, or the ability to think clearly and understand comprehensively is developed. Traditionally, two categories of this are given: 'Hearing' Wisdom* and 'Thinking' Wisdom.* The first is the accumulation of raw facts through learning while the second is the relating of them together to from new knowledge. In this way, two aspects of mental activity are developed—memory and intellectual effort. Both of these combining in mundane wisdom, are useful for the student of Dhamma. It is noteworthy that Buddhist practice does not impose any intellectual checks on its followers for it is intellect refined which is transmuted into the 'Developed' Wisdom.* Buddhists may, and indeed are, encouraged to ask any questions they wish. But Buddhists' mundane wisdom in primarily to appreciate the need to do something about their lives and so come to Practise what the Buddha has taught.

RENUNCIATION AND ITS PERFECTION

Among practices which are helpful, leading inward to the goal of Nibbana, is that connected with renunciation. Indeed this quality, whether one follows the path of homeless monks and nuns or that of householders, always forms the bedrock upon which the noble temple of the Dhamma is built in one's heart.

Renunciation should never be dreaded, for the wise see in it the greatest good. Only a person of cramped, materialist horizons dwelling in a tangle of cares and worries, fears it—and the fear is even more illusory than the affairs with which such a person is concerned. The less one is able to renounce, the less one is able to practise, and the less practice means delayed realization. The more one is able to give up, the deeper will be one's understanding and practice, and in consequence, the more thorough and speedy realization will be. It has been said that people of the 'East' are able more easily to renounce things as they have fewer of them (than westerners). But ability to renounce does not depend on geography or upon things but upon the mind. The Buddha pointed out that a man may live in a mud hut, lead a miserable life, have an ugly wife and no money but if he sees monks, even Arahants, it does not stir his mind to become like them and he clings to his misery. Another man is the son of a wealthy family, has much money and can have whatever he wants, is surrounded by beautiful companions, yet seeing those who have renounced all, he is inspired to follow their example and to become one of them. People having a Buddhist culture will be acquainted with at least some of the numerous stories of renunciation that are found in the Buddhist works connected with the past lives of the Bodhisatta who was to become Gotama the Buddha. His last life also is a very inspiring theme for renunciation.[21]

---

21. See, *The Splendour of Enlightenment —a Life of the Buddha*, (two volumes) from Mahamakut Press.

To renounce is to go the Way of Dhamma. Here Dhamma means 'the-way-things-really-are', so that neither mind nor body, nor of course things collected about them, can be thought of as belonging to a person. The Buddha frequently advised: "Do you renounce what is not yours. And what is not yours? Mind is not yours. Body is not yours." A hard teaching? Yes, but a teaching which one can put to good use in one's daily life. It makes an astonishing difference if one remembers during sickness, an accident or some emotional upset 'Mind is not mine, body is not mine.' It is like placing a soothing balm upon an open sore. Mind and body become cool and there arises detachment and equanimity which then allows a clear and just assessment of the situation, whatever it may be. This is renunciation at work, the getting rid, if only for a little time, of the troublesome and illusory 'I'.

Renunciation is thus not the forced type of New Year's Resolution in which one states firmly (for the first day at any rate) that "I will give up cigarettes... beer..." or whatever it is, this is most unrealistic and seldom works for long. Renunciation shows in the true Buddhist life because one is happy to give up a claim to ownership over what does not really belong to one.

The Perfection of Renunciation is illustrated in the story of the great King Maghadeva who renounced his throne while there were still many years of life left to him in order to take up the life of a hermit and practise meditation. But so much impressed were his people with their king's nobility of character that great numbers of them gave up their homes and wandered into the forest after him so that instead of a solitary hermitage, he lived in a village of hermits all of whom practised under his guidance and attained the fruits of the Divine Abodes and rebirth in the Realm of Subtle Form. The king was of course, a previous birth in the continuity leading up finally to the birth of Prince Siddhattha. The practice of Dhamma is ever thus: for the good of one who practises as well as leading many others to happiness.

Of course, renunciation of the household life may be accompanied, as in the case of Gotama, by renunciation of attachments, or it may not. By the Perfection of Renunciation, not only leading the homeless life is meant though conditions for practice of Dhamma are usually more favourable in the state of homelessness. What is meant by this Perfection is completeness of inward renunciation, for although outward renunciation may not be accompanied by an inward one, to find the latter without the former is unusual.

Besides the renunciation of material things with which we are not so much concerned, what is the good Buddhist to renounce? One has to be ready to give up attachment to mind and body. No empty renunciation is this, no token or symbolic renunciation but an actual practice guided by Wisdom and inspired by Compassion.

To renounce is excellent but it must be accompanied by a more positive idea of what is to be done. Hence the connection with the succeeding factor:

ASPIRATION AND ITS PERFECTION

Here it must be said that one should never undertake what is beyond one's powers to accomplish since there is nothing more frustrating than a broken aspiration. One must have the measure of one's own powers and these, it is best to consider in the beginning for reasons of humility, are frail and required constant attention to promote their growth. A person of very limited merits and strong defilements should be wise before declaring "I aspire to become an Arahant or Buddha!" Perhaps this is just megalomania and certainly it sounds like self importance! A famous Buddhist Teacher Shantideva, has written: "If one like me, still not free from the defilements, should propose to set free from the defilements the beings extending through the ten directions (of space), I should speak like a madman, ignorant of my limitations. Hence, without turning back, I shall always fight the defilements."

However, given conditions when an aspiration can be fulfilled (and aspirations connected with Giving for instance, are not usually difficult to fulfill) a Buddhist can with determination make useful progress along the Way.

It is only when one's merits are already very great that one may aspire to be one who discovers the Dhamma for himself, a Perfect Buddha. Such was the aspiration that arose in the heart of Sumedha, the brahmin ascetic when he, ages ago, first beheld the Buddha Dipamkara. While offering his body to that Buddha so that he and the attendant monks might cross a swampy place, Sumedha is said to have vowed: "Ah! May I too in some future time become a Tathagata, Arahant, a Perfect Buddha complete in clear knowledge and compassionate, conduct, supremely good in presence and in destiny, Knower of the worlds, Incomparable master of those to be tamed, Teacher of devas and humanity as this Exalted Dipamkara is now. So may I set rolling the incomparable Wheel of Dhamma as does now the Exalted Dipamkara... Having thus crossed, may I lead others across; freed may I free others; comforted, may I comfort others as this Exalted Dipamkara does now. May I become this for the happiness and welfare of humanity, out of compassion for the world, for the sake of the great multitude, for the happiness and welfare of gods and men." Sumedha was also a past birth in the series culminating in Gotama Buddha, this being the time he first aspired to Enlightenment.

We are very fortunate in that we live in the times of a Buddha, when the Dhamma of the Buddha Gotama is still well-known and practised. It is therefore unnecessary for us to aspire to become Perfect Buddhas and we should rather vow to undertake the practice of as much Dhamma as possible. We may aspire to give alms regularly, undertake and practice the Precepts, or spend so much time every day in meditation practice. The path to Enlightenment starts with very ordinary everyday things and while our aspiration may be the penetration to the Dhamma in our own hearts, we should say little about it to others.

The important thing with any aspiration is that it leads to definite Dhamma practice. By means of it one is able more easily to put down the defilements and to examine them, and to increase in all the various aspects of Dhamma. Vows are often made in front of Buddha-relics, shrines and Buddha-images. Sometimes they are undertaken in the presence of living Teachers. They must be practical to be effective.

GIVING AND ITS PERFECTION

Also called generosity this stands at the head of a path often advocated for lay Buddhist practice: Giving, Virtue and Collectedness. Why is Giving so important? If we are to make any progress along the Buddha's Way, we shall have to reverse our 'normal' worldly way. Worldliness talks about 'getting,' the Way about 'Giving.' To get more and more things means that besides becoming in the ordinary way more selfish, we are also buttressing our feelings of 'I am' with a heap of possessions which proclaim to us, and to everyone else, 'I have.' This will only lead to a fleeting worldly happiness, not to lasting happiness as the deluded suppose, and certainly not permit one to go along a spiritual way. The latter requires a strong sense of renunciation, a loosening of the bonds which bind one to things and a consequent development of the mind which will lead steadily, and surely in the direction of the knowledge that 'I am' is really false. So, the objective of Giving is to break down, or at least to make a start on the destruction of the prison walls of 'I have.' Now, Giving should be done from the heart, proceeding from a pure faith which holds that the act of giving is meritorious, that the persons to whom the giving is directed (often Buddhist monks and nuns) are pure and striving to lead a good life and that the effect upon the giver is to ensure a happy rebirth, if nothing more. In the practice of giving one should never expect any return, the only return being that one's own heart is purified, for one rejoices in a wholesome action and the heart then becomes flexible and one's ways more easy to train. What greater return could there be than this? Even if one is poor, one may still give great gifts: the gift of loving-kindness, inspiring confidence and trust in others which is for them the gift of fearlessness. Giving also includes education, merits and the Dhamma itself. It is part of the Buddhist tradition to educate well and in former times Buddhist monks were everywhere the teachers who in town and country taught the subjects then required for a good education. Actually they taught more since they themselves were a pattern for the lives of their students and thus taught them the wholesome ways of conduct which more complex modern education with its emphasis merely on acquiring facts, often fails to impart. Since Buddhist tradition has never been to lead along the blind masses in their ignorance but has always encouraged a thorough investigation, it is not surprising that many Wats or monasteries in Thailand have a school within their grounds.

Merits, as explained above cannot really 'belong' to one and merit is actually made by giving away one's merits. This is a way of teaching that one should not even be attached to the results of wholesome conduct but **using wholesome conduct**, one should push on to Nibbana, beyond both merits and demerits.

When this quality is developed to become a Perfection, it is specially characteristic of any Buddhist who has gone far along the Way. How does he give? Guided by Wisdom, which of course would guard against the giving of gifts that might cause harm, one perfected in Giving gives instantly, everything, to everybody who asks. There are again Birth-stories which illustrate this perfection excellently. Such is that of Prince Vessantara, a famous and moving story which has undoubtedly left its mark upon Buddhist culture in so many lands including Thailand, where its recitation has always been popular. The Prince proceeded to distribute largesse with such open-handedness that his ministers considered him unfit to reign. Exiled to the forest he continued to present everyone who asked with anything still left to him to give—even his wife and children who had accompanied him. While this sounds excessive to modern minds, it is said that he did so in order to prove that there was nothing that he could not renounce.

Most important is the gift of the Dhamma which excels all other gifts. Why? Because it is based on the True Nature of reality and shows all beings how they may so order their lives that instead of them being twisted by perverted thoughts, they become established upon a sure foundation of Dhamma. Through practice of the Dhamma, beings may become happy having fulfilled their various aims: Those who wish to be born again among men, for them there is the way of human Dhamma; likewise there is Dhamma for those who would prefer to go to a heavily state; and for those determined ones who aspire to be among the Ones-Who-Know, a clear Way is indicated for them as well. But to give to others such Dhamma leading to Nibbana, it is necessary to have assembled much learning, to have practised well and most necessary, to have gained insight into Nibbana for oneself.

2. VIRTUE*

PRECEPTS

The moral code of Buddhists is not an end in itself but is practised as a stepping-stone to reach Enlightenment. There are different classes of Precepts for Buddhists following the Teaching upon different levels. The Precepts are in no sense 'commandments' for no one has commanded that one should keep them: The Buddha advises us for our own happiness and for that of others that we should observe certain 'rules of training'* as the Precepts are called.

The Five Precepts* which are the basic category for lay people are all prefaced by the declaration, "I undertake the rule of training to refrain from..." The five immoral actions which lay-Buddhists train themselves to avoid are: Destroying living beings;[4] Taking what is not given; Wrong-doing in sexual desires; Speaking falsely (including lies, harsh words, tale-bearing and idle gossip); and Taking Intoxicants including drugs and those which are distilled and fermented, all being a cause for carelessness. They may be taken as a block of five together in which case if one is broken, all five are soiled; or they may be taken individually when the breaking of one does not mean that all the precepts are cancelled. In any case, whether one or all are broken, they should be renewed by taking them again, often from a monk who is one's own teacher. (In Thailand there is no difficulty as there are many monks, but in the 'West' and other places where the Order is scarce, the Precepts may be repeated by oneself, usually done in front of a Buddha-image after showing the proper marks of respect to the Teacher).

There is an idea that these are easy precepts to keep since their formulation is so brief. When however, they are explained at some length, it will be seen that 'easy' is not quite the right word for them. To illustrate this the meaning of each of the Precepts will be slightly expanded.

1. 'I undertake the rule of training to refrain from destroying living beings'—so reads the First Precept. Few people's hatred is so unrestrained that they butcher beings indiscriminately: those who do are usually confined in mental hospitals. Animal-killers such as hunters and butchers store up for themselves an unenviable and painful future as a result of their actions. Whether man or animal, one **cannot kill deliberately** without the factor of aversion (or one

22. Some bring up the old 'suppose' argument here. "Suppose that a town is infested by plague-bearing rats, does this Precept mean that a Buddhist cannot kill them?" To begin with, there is little point in arguing about statements opening with the word 'suppose' as they are hypothetical and frequently unprofitable. However, in this case the Buddhist attitude for observance of this Precepts should be clearly understood. It is good to feel shame and even an inability to kill in normal circumstances but when not only oneself but many others are threatened by death then one must use intelligence. There is no principle here to be blindly followed "that you must do this or not do that" for Buddhists, using wisdom and compassion, have themselves to decide what is the best thing to do.

of the other unwholesome roots) being active in the mind. Most people will of course say: "But I am not a maniac or a butcher" inferring thereby that they easily keep this Precept pure. They should make further enquiry: What of the fly or mosquito which so annoyed me that a heavy palm descended on it crushing its life? Flies and mosquitoes have nervous systems, they feel pain and, moreover, they want to live, not to die, as do all the animals slaughtered every day by the millions just to please humanity's tongue and belly. Then there is hunting, and mass destruction of insects, 'pests' people call them but they have a craving for life just as we have. Life is easily taken but impossible for us to give. As we do not enjoy dying ourselves, it is unwise for us to use our knowledge to destroy others.

Five factors must be present for this Precept to be broken: a living creature, awareness of its being a living creature, an intention to kill and making an effort to kill, and the death of the creature through that effort. When one of these is absent, the Precept is not broken. This applies to the factors given under the other Precepts: all of them must be present for that Precept to be called broken.

2. 'I undertake the rule of training to refrain from taking what is not given'. This is much more than not stealing. Careless borrowing for instance, will be included here when subconsciously one does not have any intention to return the article. Also, embezzlement, fraudulent business dealings and the adulteration of food, which some shopkeepers and merchants practise, should be included. The under-payment of employees is another case where this Precept is broken.

As one wishes others to respect those things which one considers as one's own, it is better to be perfectly straight with what belongs to others. This Precept is broken when the following five factors are all present: that which is owned by another, an awareness of that fact, an intention to steal, making an effort for this, and obtaining the thing through effort.

3. 'I undertake the rule of training to refrain from wrong-doing

in sexual desires.' This is often translated as refraining from adultery, a very potent cause of sorrow, not only to those who commit it but also to the faithful member of a marriage. The sorrows of the guilty parties may not be immediately obvious but the sorrows of the innocent are immediate and often disastrous. Much anguish, even suicide and mental unbalance, would be avoided if this Precept was better kept. There are also the sorrows of children in such broken marriages. The loss of one parent frequently leaves a deep scar upon young minds and may be the cause of much trouble in their later lives. Then there are economic difficulties which may come about when marriages are broken in this way. A whole heap of dukkha is caused just because men and women cannot keep in check their desire for sexual pleasures and do not have contentment, the positive counterpart of this Precept, with their marriage partner.

All sorts of other misbehaviour are also included here: rape, sexual abuse of children, while young unmarried people should wisely restrain themselves and not get involved in anything which may prove a bondage for them. Restraint is good, and it should be restraint not merely of repressing outward action, but of lustful desire, counted in Buddhist teaching among the unwholesome mental factors. When the following factors, four in number, are seen to be present then one knows that one has broken this Precept: "that which should not be gone to" (= 3 classes of woman: those married, in the care of parents, or nuns and other celibates. Or, married men, those protected by parents, or monks, novices and other celibates), an intention to practise (coition), an effort to accomplish this and permissive connection through the genital organs (with the above classes of persons).

4. 'I undertake the rule of training to refrain from false speech.' This is one of the most difficult of Precepts for people to keep, as it includes not only lying but harsh speech, backbiting and idle gossip. The tongue is not so easily kept in check, especially when one is upset, and the less it is checked, the more dukkha both oneself and others will have. Lying itself has some subtle shades not easily

distinguished unless one is very honest with oneself. Harsh speech is indulged in when angry and one blames, grumbles at, or openly abuses others, possibly using swear-words of unsavoury meaning. Those little and so interesting stories one likes to relate about other' faults, how sweet to do so and how much others enjoy listening: this is backbiting. Last, but not least, is the time-wasting idle chatter about little nothings which are scarcely worthy of words: human beings should put the precious treasure of speech and also fleeting time to better use.

Damage is done to oneself by not restraining the tongue: others will think that one is untrustworthy, violent, cunning, or a fool, while they also suffer from any violation of this Precept. It is broken in the presence of the following three factors: an intention to speak falsely, an effort to do so, and an understanding by others of what has been said.

5. 'I undertake the rule of training to refrain from distilled and fermented drinks and from drugs that cause carelessness.'[23] This precept is broken upon the coming together of these four factors: presence of intoxicants; an intention to consume it; making an effort to do so; and the act of drinking, (smoking, injecting, etc.).

All the above four Precepts depend for their purity, upon constant vigilance and if the mind is overcome by intoxicants, then what harm may not result?

A Tibetan tale is told about this:

It appears that a man of that country had aroused the enmity of

---

23. It is significant that all substances producing a distortion of normal human experience find a place under the Fifth Precept. In India, both ancient and modern, the use of drugs to stimulate 'religious' experiences including visual and auditory hallucinations, has been and is very well known and quite widely practised. The 'insights' claimed by some who in the present day take LSD etc., should be tested against the difference which these experiences make to the forces of greed, aversion and delusion in their hearts and conduct. Particularly if it is claimed that these drugs offer a kind of shortcut to Enlightenment, it must be stressed that no shortcut of this sort is possible and such experience cannot replace effort spread over many years or even over lives.

some demon. This being plagued him and told him that he would only leave him in peace if the man consented to break one of the Five Precepts.

Now that man was a sincere Buddhist layman who had successfully kept his precepts pure. He thought: 'I cannot break the first for to kill a being is a most terrible thing. As to the second, I have never stolen anything and it is a great crime. I have always been faithful to my wife and we are happy together, so how can I break the third one? Then the fourth if I break it, is sure to make someone unhappy and bring myself a bad name. What about the fifth, hmm...?' And he decided that one little drop of liquor would not do any harm and would at the same time, satisfy that demon.

He had never before tasted alcohol and the little drop that he sipped intrigued him by its taste. He thought: 'This tastes good, a little more won't harm me.' And so, a little more, and more...until he was rolling drunk. Passing a tinker on his way home, he snatched some trinkets. Reaching his house at last, he found his wife absent and noticed for the first time how pretty his neighbour's wife appeared. Going to her, he gave her the ornaments and they entered her house. After some time she proposed some food, so he took an axe and hacked off a goat's head. Finally, the tinker came up with officials to accuse him of the theft, and he denied it, loudly declaring his innocence.

And so all the five precepts were broken...

Keeping these Precepts pure is the mark of a real human being and of one who, in the event of not accomplishing anything greater will certainly be reborn as a human well-endowed with happiness and wealth. Those humans whose standard of conduct is not maintained fairly consistently at the level of the Five Precepts, do not qualify for human birth as their minds tend towards the sub-human. The effect of keeping these precepts is to remove the tensions and conflicts which so often exist between 'what I should do' (to conduct myself as a human being) and 'what I actually do' (descending to animal behaviour, etc.). Sincerely trying to perfect these Precepts, the gap between these two is removed and as a result, instead of much energy being wasted in the warfare of mental conflicts, one experiences a greater sense of tranquillity, of well-being.

Taking these Precepts proceeded by the Three Refuges, constitutes the simple ceremony in which one declares oneself a follower of Buddha-dhamma.[24] With the Three Refuges one establishes one's faith in the Teacher, the Teaching and those who have been taught, and then taking upon oneself the Five Precepts. one takes the first step towards establishing those Three Refuges of faith as Three Jewels of inward understanding. The Five precepts are the first indispensable step for reaching the ultimate goal of Enlightenment.

BASES OF VIRTUE

At one time philosophers declared that Virtue was an impossibility unless given by a creator in the form of commandments: as without either fear of their Maker or his commands, it was argued that man would run wild, become bestial. As Buddhism recognizes no Supreme Being and therefore no commandments from him, the question arises as to why moral precepts are kept by Buddhists. That they are kept is substantiated by the happiness of the Thai people and many other Buddhists, a fact which so much impresses foreigners. Such happiness comes from maintaining a good standard of morality not only in this life but is also the result of wholesome action in past existences.

Buddhist ethics are founded upon two pairs of principles: To counteract the influence of the Roots of unwholesomeness one should develop two wholesome factors in one's character: **shame and fear of evil.*** Shame is the knowing that what one does is not pure whether in mind, speech or body. The actions arising from the defilements are stained or impure. This shame is compared to a

24. See Appendix Two for a detailed explanation.

young man or woman fond of adornment around whose neck a corpse is hung.

The other factor, fear of evil, stops the making of evil kamma by considering the fearful results which will have to be borne by oneself. It is an inward fear of consequences based upon an understanding of the law of kamma. This is compared to the fear which arises at the sight of a poisonous snake.

These two are called the 'World-guardians'* for when they are present strongly in the hearts of people, no evil is done and since virtue is established by them, the world is well-protected and beings live in peace and happiness. When these World-guardians are not strengthened moral conduct degenerates, people becoming animals and worse.

The second pair are **wisdom** and **compassion**.* In this case wisdom means: clearly understanding what benefits and what harms oneself. Suppose that one is doubtful about some action; is it or is it not according to the practice of virtue? Then one should examine in this way: If I abstain from doing this, how will this benefit my mental state? If one decides that the mind will become clearer and the heart cooler, then it is proper to abstain. Or another examination may be made: If I do this what obstructions, worries or defilements will arise in my mind? After examining the mind and seeing that a certain action will bring more of dukkha, one should be wise and know what to do. Wisdom is concerned with knowing the effect of moral and immoral conduct upon oneself.

The second of this pair, compassion, is concerned with feeling for other beings. One sees that beings are suffering enough already and that the wholesome thing to do is to give aid, certainly not breaking the Precepts which will only make them more miserable. Buddhist compassion is not only sympathizing with the sufferings of others, a rather passive attitude, but it is actively making an effort to remove those sufferings. Hence the Buddhist practice particularly stressed in Thailand called the Five Ennobling Virtues*or the positive counterparts of the Five Precepts. They can hardly be practised though, before Precepts of abstention are well-established. They are: Friendliness/Compassion, Right Livelihood, Contentment, Truthfulness, and Mindfulness all of which are described elsewhere in this book.

Without pure Virtue, it is dangerous to practise Collectedness (Meditation) and doubtful in any case, whether much could ever come of such practice. Unless the basis of uprightness in moral matters has been made secure, it is impossible to realize Supermundane Wisdom and Freedom. Thus the attainment of the very goal of Buddhist endeavour depends upon sustained effort to maintain and to strengthen the emotional attitude of nonviolence, to oneself and to others.

It has been emphasized already that moral activity of this sort should pervade all aspects of one's life. In speech, this is guaranteed by keeping the Fourth Precept unbroken and moral bodily action is ensured by the practice of the first three Precepts. It only remains to note that Lord Buddha also emphasized the need for purity in livelihood. He declared that his followers should abstain from these ways of earning a living: Dealing in weapons (arms-sales are big money in our world!), trading in living beings, (as slaves and making money from prostitutes, as well as selling animals into bondage), in meats (as this involves the killing of animals), in liquor or drugs, (as we have seen in the tale, when all the first four Precepts are easily broken), in poisons (when sold for the purpose of killing). If restraint in these matters and other harmful kinds of livelihood was well observed in this world, no one can deny that it would be a much happier and more peaceful place in which to live.

Besides the Five Precepts just mentioned, reference must be made briefly to some others. On Full Moon, New Moon and two quarter-moon intermediate holy-days in the lunar month, devoted Buddhists go to their temples and declare their wish to practise extra Precepts. These are the Eight Precepts* formed by converting the third of the Five into "refraining from all sexual actions" and then adding three more: to refrain from seeing shows, dances and all sorts of entertainments and not to adorn or perfume one's body, and not to sleep on a soft or luxurious bed. These are generally observed by devotees for one day after which they take back upon themselves the Five Precepts. While they are practising the Eight, they have a chance to stay in some quiet place, often in a monastery and there devote their time to meditation, study or listening to the teaching of monks, all of which may be difficult for them to do at other times. If these precepts are undertaken regularly, the mental level is definitely improved and the rebirth traditionally resulting from their practice is to arise among the gods of Sensual Desire.

Slightly more rigorous are the Ten Precepts* binding on a Novice.* The former Eight are made into nine by splitting the Precept on shows and ornaments and one other is added: to refrain from handling gold and silver. By this is meant of course, money. Monks and novices who are strict in their practice of the Teaching do not give themselves the chance to handle is simply by never possessing it. It is very wholesome to have the experience of being without money, for while one has it, desires may be gratified and one suffers from the delusion that money, in buying things one wants, also buys happiness. When one is without money, it is then necessary to fall back upon one's own skills, and where these do not provide what is needed, to cultivate that excellent virtue-contentment. This is of course specially for the monk's or nun's way of life and is not meant to be observed by laypeople. At the age of twenty, a novice may become a monk and in doing so, agrees to strive to observe the 227 Precepts of his special code into which the above Ten precepts are incorporated. We shall not describe these, the first four having been mentioned already. It is worth noting that seventy-five of these rules are concerned with good manners and correct deportment. Undoubtedly, these Precepts have had their effect upon the politeness, not only to be found among the monks but also among Thai lay people, for foreigners coming mostly into contact with them, are frequently impressed by their courtesy.

PERFECTION OF VIRTUE

This Perfecting Quality which eventually becomes an integral part
of the Enlightened person is the last part of a long course of training.
Training in moral conduct must always start with oneself for if one
has trained oneself, others will naturally follow the admirable
example that they see. When a great deal of self-training has been
accomplished, it is said that one fails in the Perfection of Virtue if
one neglects to guide others in the observance of morality. In
Buddhist tradition this is always done by example and can never be
accomplished by empty exhortations, promises or warnings.

Buddhist tradition declares that moral conduct (as understood in
Dhamma) is the hallmark of true spiritual attainment. A very good
way to examine those in this world who claim to be religious teachers
is to observe closely their moral conduct. If their lapses of virtue
(as manifestations of Greed, Aversion and Delusion) are said by such
people either to be unimportant at their stage of spirituality, or else
that they are meant as tests for the faith of followers, one may then
know such teachers' to be either deluded by conceit, downright
frauds, or among those unfortunate individuals with a dual or 'split'
personality. The doctrine that 'The Saint is above sin though his
actions may be sin for worldly men' finds no support in the
Dhamma, where the Arahant, who has destroyed greed, Aversion
and Delusion is incapable of: "intentionally destroying a living
being; of taking by way of theft what is not given; of practising the
sexual act; of telling a deliberate lie; of indulging in intoxicants; of
storing up food for the indulgence of appetite as he did before when
a householder; of taking a wrong course through aversion; of taking
a wrong course through delusion; and of taking a wrong course
through fear."

Backsliding at any stage of developing this quality, whether in the
ordinary way or as a Perfection, always leads to a collapse of whatever
has been accomplished already and hence is always blamed. The
Bodhisatta, as related in the Birth Stories, usually maintained a high

level of virtue, though occasionally he too slipped and had to suffer the results of his kamma.

The classical story illustrating this Perfection is that of Bhuridatta, king of the legendary serpent-spirits of great powers. Vowing upon one Observance Day to keep the Eight Precepts, he lay down by an anthill in his serpent form. A snake-catcher seeing his great size and beauty captured and then maltreated him Even though as the story relates, one glance of his would have been sufficient to reduce his tormentor to ashes, he bore the pain and fixed his mind upon the pure observance of the Precepts. Gotama the Buddha is said to have been in a previous birth that Naga-king Bhuridatta and to have thus completed his training in the Perfection of Virtue.

As the preceding pages have shown, though very briefly, the practice of Virtue consists, in the Dhamma, of dynamic 'ways of training' leading forward not merely to an increase of happiness here, but much more important, to the successful practice of Collectedness, with which the next few pages will be concerned.

3. COLLECTEDNESS (OR 'MEDITATION')*

'Meditation' is an inadequate rendering of several more precise terms in Pali and Sanskrit. The nearest equivalents to some of these in English would be: (mental) development,* one-pointedness,* collectedness,* (absorbed) concentration.* From these we may gain some idea of the sort of range of Buddhist 'meditation'. This word has therefore been replaced in favour of the more accurate 'collectedness'.

DEFINITION OF MEDITATION

Collectedness as practised by the Buddha and the disciples who have followed him, may be summed up as 'one-pointedness of mind', a condition which is not attained by most people without a great deal of effort. The ordinary person supposes, as there is little evidence to the contrary, that the world perceived is the only one: collectedness on the other hand, if it is practised will show that the spiritual universe is very much greater than ordinary thought conceives. Is it then to attain such knowledge that Buddhists practise meditation? The answer is 'No' if one aspires to Nibbana but some not upon the direct path do aspire for heavenly existence. In either case it is for stilling the mind's restless wandering so that the grosser mental hindrances* (Sense Desire, Ill-will, Sloth and Torpor, Restlessness and Worry, and Scepticism), are removed. The ordinary person's mind may be compared to a pond of muddy water ruffled unceasingly by a strong wind. When one enters a state of collectedness and the senses are withdrawn from their objects, the wind of desire is stilled. When this happens, the ripples of hindrances cease to disturb the mind. The mind is now like a calm but still muddy pond. This condition does, however, give one a chance to develop Wisdom. This is like alum crystals which will clear the pool, making it pellucid, so that even the smallest objects upon its bottom may be seen in every detail. For this reason ultimately, collectedness is practised, as Wisdom is the key to Enlightenment.[25]

25. The time has come perhaps, to note a few of the mistaken notions concerning what is meant by 'meditation' in Buddhism. Quite definitely, it is not 'Doing nothing' as anyone who tries it will find out. Just because a person's body is not jigging around and 'doing something,' some have supposed that a meditator is just excusing himself to take a rest or a little sleep on the quiet. This belief is best broken by practice! Others think that 'Meditation' is dreaming. In dream-states the mind slips downwards and loses mindfulness. The Concentrations, as have been pointed out, are characterized by a vastly increased power of mindfulness. Another popular notion about meditation is that is consists of making the mind blank, quite untrue since the perfectly meditative mind always has something it knows. Meditation experience is something very wonderful and not at all associated with grey dullness. Auto-hypnosis was another scholar's 'explanation' of Buddhist meditation. Needless to say, that scholar had never practised it. Hypnotic states, like dreams, are definitely without any mindfulness. Another person thought, more reasonably, that meditation is like discursive prayer. Although there are discursive

Before a concentration of mind can be experienced, the two great hindrances which stand blocking the way of the meditator like Scylla and Charybdis, must be carefully circumnavigated. These are sleepiness, slothfulness with its resulting unworkability of the mind, and the opposite hindrance of the 'monkey-mind' which restlessly clambers about from one object to another. Two things will happen when a person starts to take interest in mind-training and actually sits down to try to practise: either dozing off, waking after some time with a dull feeling, remembering nothing; or else the mind will seem like an uncontrollable fountain of words, ideas, plans, pictures and memories, all demanding attention. These are the two great obstacles to attainment. How strong they are, or which one is stronger in any one character, can only be discovered from actual practice. The definite attainment of a Concentration means that one has broken through the desire 'barrier' and penetrated to a different realm of things—the Realm of Subtle Form. The (absorbed) Concentrations, four of them correspond of the four great levels of that heavenly realm, and are characterized by varying intensities of the following spiritual factors: Mindfulness, Happiness, Joy, One-pointedness and Equanimity.

MENTAL FACTORS OF COLLECTEDNESS

Mindfulness* plays a very important part in the Buddhist Way, not only in sitting practice but also in daily life. In the latter it is the quality of carefulness, both in respect of things such as possessions or the actions of one's body, and of mental states, as when a Buddhist guards himself with mindfulness so that unwholesome states decline or are not permitted to arise and the wholesome are increased and made stable. Buddhists are taught in great detail what to be mindful of: the body, its movements and positions, its

---

meditations in Buddhist practice, one-pointed meditation aims at the elimination, not encouragement, of the constant stream of words flowing through the mind.

impermanence and decay, its patchwork nature; of the feelings: pleasant, painful and neither-pleasant-nor-painful; of the moods of the mind; and of particular groups of factors which it is useful to identify for one's growth in Dhamma.

As a factor of meditative states, mindfulness is intensified to become that quality which does not permit mind to wander from one object on to another, even when concentration has become most subtle. It is therefore, quite invaluable for the attainment of any sort of mind-concentration. Only of mindfulness has the Buddha said: "This is the path going in one way for the purification of beings, for the overcoming of sorrow and lamentation, for the destruction of pain and grief, for reaching the right path, for realization of Nibbana…"

Happiness and joy* are the best that language can do to describe experiences of subtle bliss. Both factors have to be abandoned by one who would progress to even finer states of meditation, a difficult thing if one has experienced these states. Indeed many meditators get stuck at this point assuming that this blissful peace is the highest possible attainment. This is the 'union with God' experience of meditators from different religious traditions. It is also the source for the feeling of 'oneness with nature' which is extolled by nature mystics. None of such experiences have anything to do with Enlightenment which must be sought through insight into the nature of one's mind and body.

One-pointedness signifies that only one object concerns the mind during its attainment of these states. It does not wander here and there as it is accustomed to do 'normally'. Before Concentration can be experienced it is necessary that one-pointedness is easily maintained.

Equanimity* here means the perfect balance of the mental condition finally attained in the fourth of the Concentrations. With mindfulness and equanimity perfectly cultured in the mind, two further directions are open to the meditator. One may either ascend the infinitude of the Formless Realm or one may develop the Magical Abilities.*

MAGICAL ABILITIES

The former have already been touched upon but a few words would be appropriate on the latter. These Abilities[26] are the basis of all the 'miracles' so prominent in many religious teachers' lives. They are found too, in connection with the Buddha, his disciples and his tradition to the present day. The difference between their occurrence in non-Buddhist traditions and in Dhamma, is that in the former, they are seen to be mysterious manifestations of some other power appearing to operate only among those to whom God gives them. In the latter it is noteworthy that the Buddha rarely used them and then only for some very good purpose. They are a part of mind development which anyone sufficiently persevering may experience. While Dhamma can point out clear methods to obtain these powers, practicers are warned that they should attach little importance to them, in fact, better disregard them altogether. For a Buddhist, the mind is the seat of all troubles, but by practice it can become the place of Enlightenment. Instead of pruning the twigs of the craving creeper with these Abilities one should get to the bottom and chop at the root with the axe of Wisdom.

TWO STREAMS IN MIND-DEVELOPMENT

Before mental development and character-types are discussed in the section below, collectedness can be classified on the basis of practice. Two apparently distinct streams may be seen though when collectedness is established they are seen to be complementary.

---

26. Buddhist collectedness should not be practised to gain these. They maybe won as the fruits of much meditative toil but their use is discouraged by the words of the Buddha. They are, of course, very interesting. They are the basis for all the tales told of 'magical' occurrences, but they are very dangerous indeed in the hands of anyone who has not developed wisdom. An ordinary person who acquires them will certainly become conceited and probably use them for selfish purposes, or else out of spite use them against others, as was the case with the Buddha's cousin, Devadatta.

It is best for some people whose minds are very active and who incline to suffer from distraction, to follow with mindfulness the mad monkey-mind's acrobatics. As the mind is really a series of mental events which arise and pass away with great rapidity, each of which is a mind complete with supporting mental factors, so at the beginning this kind of mindfulness is really one's 'mindful' minds watching other 'minds' (which are all within one's own mental continuity of course). One thereby develops the ability to look into the mind and to see where it has gone to. Has it gone to the past, present or future? Has it gone to body, or to feelings, or perhaps to memories, to thoughts, or has it gone to consciousness? By this method of 'Where has it gone?' the distracted mind slowly comes under the surveillance of the mindful mind until mindfulness forms a strong foundation for further development. when the mind has become calm, one should start to practise for the development of the Concentrations which will in their turn be the basis for the arising of real insight. This method is called wisdom-leading-to-calm.

Other methods suited to those whose minds are less disturbed initially include the classic forty subjects of meditation (see below for some of them) and these, together with some other devices, involve the use of a definite object for concentration. This may be one's own body or a part of it, a colour or a picture, a word or a phrase, an abstract contemplation and so forth. When we say 'object' it should be understood that this means something in one's self, not an object 'out there'. All these methods involve some gentle discipline of the mind in that each time it strays away, it must be gently brought back again (by mindfulness of course) to concentrate again on the chosen object.

All the subjects listed below are of this second type in which the calm gained from practice is then used for the arousing of wisdom. For this reason they are called calm-leading-to-wisdom methods and are very necessary in the present distracted age.

MIND-DEVELOPMENT AS MEDICINE

Collectedness in the Buddhist tradition is like medicine: as the body has certain illnesses and requires different drugs for its cure, so the different unwholesome mental states require different meditative treatment. It is difficult for people to decide by themselves which disease affects them or into which character-group they fall, which is one reason why collectedness is usually only practised with the aid of a teacher who is qualified to judge one's character and prescribe for it accordingly. In addition, one's character is not a stable 'being' but an ever-changing series of processes. Meditation methods guide that change and sometimes require changing themselves as one's mental state makes this necessary. Again, a teacher is essential for guidance. Finally, most people are not rooted in only one type of character but are a mixture, in which different roots become predominant at different times. Below is given one of the best-known and most ancient character-classifications set out about 1,500 years ago by a great teacher-monk, Buddhaghosa. It is not intended to be all-inclusive but is designed specially for meditative purposes:

	CHARACTERS ROOTED IN	MEDITATIONS SUITABLE
Three Roots of Unwhole-someness	Greed*	Decay of the Body 32 Parts of the Body Loathsomeness of Food
	Aversion*	Loving-kindness: (suitable for all)
	Delusion*	Conditioned Arising of Dhammas
	Faith	Qualities of the Dhamma
	Intelligence*	Qualities of the Buddha .
	Discursiveness*	Mindfulness of Breathing: (suitable for all)

With training, Greed-rooted characters cease to centre their greed upon themselves and then lavish devotion upon their ideal. They then become Faith-rooted but require learning and wisdom to balance their spiritual growth. To divert the energies of greed to more wholesome channels, the body's 32 messy bits and pieces* are systematically brought to mind, and meditated upon until they are actually seen with meditative vision. Having done this, one relinquishes greediness for what is after all a mass of blood, skin and bones, etc., and ceases to identify oneself with this body. It is also useful to cut down one's attachment to food by seeing it not as tasty, good-smelling, agreeably textured, etc., but to get at the bare impression of that food which the senses receive before one's mental processes colour the whole issue with greed.[27] Thus, these meditations are expedient means to unwrap Greed from its objects and so make possible an expansion of the mind's range on to objects spiritual.

The Faith-character, in the chart on page 106, has a meditation which, when it is well-developed, will cause him to gain considerable Wisdom as balance for his character. The actual meaning of Qualities of the Dhamma are not explained here in detail though a brief list is given: **Svakkhato Bhagavata dhammo**, (the Dhamma of the Blessed One is perfectly expounded), **sanditthiko** (to be seen

27. Neither these practices nor any others used in Buddhism, are to be compared with the flagellations, hair shirts and other self-torture sometimes recommended in or practised by those following other religions. In such religions, the body is something distinct from mind and it tends to become, in the hands of religious fanatics, a good whipping post for troubles, the sources of which are really mental. However, this is not perceived and so 'Brother Ass' is variously subjected to discomforts with the very mistaken notion of 'mortification of the flesh.' The body has no desires!

Mind and body are in Buddhist practice and for practical considerations, sometimes dealt with separately but it is recognized that they are a complex, one reacting upon the other. It is usual in Buddhism to work directly upon the mind rather than use bodily measures to control the mind, though the Buddha did allow thirteen mildly ascetic Practices for the restraint of the body, (see, *With Robes and Bowl*, in Books by the Same Author).

here and now), **akaliko** (not a matter of time), **ehipassiko** (inviting one to come and see), **opanayiko**, (leading inward), **paccattam veditabbo vinnuhiti** (to be known by the wise, each for themselves). These are the profound Qualities of his Teaching which the Buddha has declared.

The Aversion-dominated type, has to develop, in spite of a difficult character, the quality of Friendliness. It is helpful for its development if one treats objects with care and mindfulness, dwells in a place where people do not arouse anger and so gradually learns patience and gentleness. An Aversion-type is sharp in seeing things unlovely, unlikeable but with practice, may change this unhealthy characteristic to sharpness in seeing the meanings in Dhamma. One has then changed to become one rooted in intelligence. A person of this sort tends to be intellectually gifted but emotionally rather dry. S/he needs a meditation which awakens particularly the balancing emotion of faith. This is provided by the meditation on the Qualities of the Buddha:

Itipi so Bhagava (Indeed the Blessed One is thus): **Araham** (the accomplished destroyer of defilements), **Sammasambuddho** (a Buddha perfected by himself). **Vijjacaranasampanno** (complete in clear knowledge and compassionate conduct), **Sugato** (supremely good in presence and in destiny), **Lokavidu** (Knower of the worlds), **Anuttaro purisadammasarathi** (incomparable master of those to be trained), **Sattha devamanussanam** (Teacher of devas and humanity), **Buddho**, (Awakened and Awakener) **Bhagavati** (and the Lord by skillful means apportioning Dhamma). Dwelling upon this one comes to understand that in the person of the Buddha, one has not the benevolent old ascetic of some writers, not Gotama the man, not the rationalist, nor yet an emanation of a Godhead: one has before one in this contemplation, Gotama the Perfectly Enlightened who won Nibbana, a state beyond all discriminations (see III). A great sense of reverence is awakened by this practice, reverence which passes into devotion as one comes not merely to believe, but to understand, and from understanding in turn, humility is born.

This last factor is most essential for intellectuals who easily imagine
that they understand Buddhism. With them, it is as though they
mistook a drop of orange juice for the whole contents of the orange,
which they have not yet begun to peel. The attitude of falsely
supposing that one knows all about it is easily dispelled from looking
at one's own life—is it perfected yet? How concentrated is one's
mind? How tranquil is one's collectedness? Real understanding of
Dhamma, not to be got merely from books, lectures or reflection, is
only arrived at after considerable and persistent practice.

The person in whom the last of the Three Roots of Unwholesomeness is strong suffers from the inability to understand, from
dullness, from blockages in the mental works which only permit
the wheels to grind on slowly. The meditation required is one which
will awaken intelligence and for this, simple applications of the
Dependant Arising of all dhammas (events) will prove helpful. In
its simplest form the formula, already mentioned, runs thus: "This
being, that becomes; from the cessation of this, that ceases."* This
is the basis of Buddhist thought, this is the great fundamental insight
of the Buddha as taught by one of his earliest disciples:

> *Whatever events arising from a cause*
> *The Tathagata has told the cause of them*
> *And of their cessation too,*
> *The Great Monk teaches thus.*

Take any object: a tree, a cloud, an ant, and finally consider the
human mind and body. All these 'events' (dhammas) arise
conditionally, exist conditionally, and pass away conditionally.
What is said of the world of outer sense-impressions is also true of
the functions of the mind. Mental states and mental processes arise
due to certain conditions and pass away as those conditions pass
away. We see again processes at work and through meditating upon
them, Wisdom arises thus clearing away the gloom of dullness.

The last of the character-types is similar to the deluded person as both delusion and discursiveness have the inability to penetrate a subject. In the former case however, dullness prevented understanding. While in the latter the latter the mind, often bright, has a momentary interest in subjects and then drops them, being incapable of persistent concentration. Such a person often has a wide accumulation of facts but is unable to relate them together and therefore has no depth of understanding. This combination of intelligence and instability calls for a practice which slows down the mind's butterfly movements and brings deep concentration. Such a meditation is Mindfulness of Breathing*[28] in which the in and out breaths are watched with mindfulness, usually concentrated upon the tip of the nose, though different teachers have their own methods. This method will bring peace and therefore greater understanding in its wake, much to the advantage of the discursive character.

Regarding the relation of the two great hindrances, sloth and restlessness, to these different characters, the former will tend to be experienced by those rooted most strongly in Greed, in Faith and in Delusion. The remaining three characters are sharper and their particular hindrance in mind-development is the devil of distraction.

As to the actual methods of practice, they have not been much explained in this introductory book. The amount of information about these and the numerous other meditation techniques is very great, Buddhists having made a special study of this branch of religious lore for the past twenty-five centuries. Those who are interested to try for themselves the advantages of a tamed mind, having gone for Refuge to the Buddha, Dhamma and Sangha, should find and then approach a good teacher of the subject, requesting him with the traditional formalities to accept one as a

28. This should not be confused with the yogic forced-breathing practices. The latter should never be taken up without an expert teacher, and while the writer would not generally counsel anyone to practise meditation without a guide, this Mindfulness of Breathing will not lead to any harmful results providing one does no try to force the pace. The meditation on Loving-kindness can also be practiced by everyone.

pupil. Then, revering him and his instructions, for to the pupil he stands now in place of the Buddha, one should diligently put the latter into practice. After this, instead of reading books about Dhamma one may come to realize its truths in one's own heart.

PRACTICAL ADVICE FOR MEDITATORS

Turning from the psychological to the practical aspect, meditation (collectedness) for laypeople may be divided into two categories: that which is done intensively and that which one practises while going about one's daily life. The meditation practised intensively is also of two sorts: regular daily sitting, and occasional periodic practice. We shall first discuss the regular period of sitting which should, where possible, be made every day at the same time. One should guard against it becoming a ritual by earnestness and being intensely aware of why one has undertaken it. The following suggestions may be found helpful as well.

As to material considerations, the place for meditation should be fairly quiet. If one has a small room which can be used only for this purpose, so much the better. It is best to meditate alone unless other members of the household also practise. Where this is the case one should make sure that one's mind is pure and even in respect of others, for otherwise greed, aversion and the rest of the robber-gang are sure to steal away the fruits of meditation.

Quietness is best obtained by getting up early before others rise and this is also the time when the mind is clear and the body rested. Sincere meditators try to keep regular hours for they know how much depends on having just enough sleep to feel refreshed. After rising and washing, sit down in clean loose clothing in the meditation place. One may have a small shrine with Buddhist symbols but this is not essential. Some people find it useful to begin by making the offerings of flowers, incense and light (see Part I), carefully reflecting while doing so. It is very common in Buddhist countries to preface one's silent meditation by chanting softly to oneself "**Namo tassa bhagavato Arahato Sammasambuddhassa**" with the Refuges and the Precepts (see Appendix Two where all this is explained).

Another useful preliminary is a discursive meditation in Pali and English, or just in English, upon Loving-Kindness:

Aham sukhito homi—May I be happy; **niddukkho homi**—may I be free from suffering; **avero homi**—may I be free from enmity; **abyapajjho homi**—may I be free from hurtfulness; **anigho homi**—may I be free from troubles of mind and body; **sukhi attanam pariharami**—may I be able to protect my own happiness. **Sabbe satta**—Whatever beings there are: **sukhita hontu**—may they be happy; **sabbe satta**—whatever beings there are: **niddukkha hontu**—may they be free from suffering; **sabbe satta**—whatever beings there are: **avera hontu**—may they be free from enmity; **sabbe satta**—whatever beings there are: **abyapajjha hontu**—may they be free from hurtfulness; **sabbe satta**—whatever beings there are: **anigha hontu**—may they be free from troubles of mind and body; **sabbe satta**—whatever beings there are: **sukhi attanam pariharantu**—may they be able to protect their own happiness.

When sitting, care should be taken to be at once relaxed yet holding the body erect. There should be no strain but neither should the head droop nor the lumber regions sag. The body should feel poised and balanced upright. Although the cross-legged positions (such as the lotus posture) are best with the meditator seated on a fairly soft mat, a chair may be used by those unaccustomed to the lotus posture or else unable to train themselves to sit in that way. Sitting in lotus posture (or half-lotus) will be found much easier if a rather hard cushion is placed so as to raise the buttocks. The knees will then tend to touch the ground and a firm three-pointed sitting (two knees and buttocks) is then attained.

One should sit for the same length of time every day until, as one becomes more proficient in collecting the mind, automatically one will feel like extending the practice. One widely-used method for measuring the meditation period is sitting for the length of time taken for a stick of incense to burn down. Having placed the hands in meditation posture relaxed in the lap, the eyes may be closed or left slightly open according to whatever is found most comfortable.

Methods used for helping to concentrate the mind are many and a few of the classical meditations have been briefly reviewed in the section above. Other helpful methods include the repetition of a word or series of them and perhaps with it the use of a rosary. If one practises mindfulness of breathing, some may find the use of a word such as "Bud-dho," or "Ara-ham" good for quietening the mind. The first syllable is silently repeated when breathing in while one concentrates on the second during the out-breathing. When the meditation is on a series of words, a rosary may be used, each repetition marked by one bead, as when, for instance, repeating the qualities of the Buddha or Dhamma.

One's meditation goes well if one finds the mind increasingly absorbed on the chosen meditation subject but one should not assume that meditation is useless just because for months little but sleepiness or distractions are experienced. For success, great persistence and evenness of effort are necessary.

The meditation period may close with some chanting, the usual subject being the well-being of others and the dedication of merits to them. The translation below from the Pali verses by the great Buddhist King Mongkut (Rama IV of Siam) could be used:

> *May the merits made by me*
> *now or at some other time*
> *Be shared among all beings here*
> *infinite, immeasurable.*
> *By rejoicing in this cause,*
> *this gift of merit given by me*
> *May beings all forever live*

a happy life, be free from hate
And may they find the Path Secure
and their good wishes all succeed!

As regards chanting, it is very useful to know a few Discourses of the Buddha in Pali, or in English translation and to use these for collecting the mind if there should be an occasion when no concentration at all can be obtained. At such a time a meditator should not feel depressed but should continue sitting and chant softly. This is what many Buddhist monks do twice a day as part of their Dhamma-practice and it is useful as well for fostering a more devotional approach necessary as a balance to insight meditation. Another useful method for the overcoming of distraction is walking-practice which may be done in any passage or in a secluded walk in the garden. A length of twenty or thirty paces will be sufficient for if longer the mind tends to wander and if shorter, distraction may be increased. One should walk at the speed one feels natural with the hands clasped in front of the body and keep one's mind fixed upon one's subject of meditation, or just upon the movement of the legs and the touch of the feet on the ground.

If one is not too tired after work and if there is the opportunity in the evening, another period of sitting can be undertaken then. In any case, before sleep, it is good to sit if only for a few minutes so as to purify the mind before lying down. One may consider thus: 'When I lie down there is no certainty that I shall awake! One may therefore be lying down to die, a good reflection to rouse wholesome states of mind and banish sensual unwholesome ones. If one practises 'the lying-down to die,' it will be a very good preparation for the real event which is bound to take place at some time in the unknown future. It may even generate the right conditions for the arising of insight, allowing one 'to die' giving up the grasping of what does not belong to one, that is, the mind and body. At this time also, a Dhamma phrase or word may be used repeating which one eventually falls to sleep. In this way one ends and begins the day with practice of Buddhist Teachings and apart from devotion of one's whole day to them, what could be better?

Regarding the second division of intensive practice, that is, meditation retreat, much will depend upon what facilities are available to the earnest student. There are now a few places in the West where meditation instruction can be sought. The most important thing is to have direct contact with an able meditation teacher (books only serve at the beginning, while even an interpreter is later found deficient in some way). After satisfying this one condition, only one other is necessary: one must strive with diligence to practise and realize the teachings. If these two conditions are fulfilled then one is the most fortunate among human beings.

Many will be without access to a Teacher and some may like to try a period of solitary meditation in some quiet part of the country. This should only be attempted if one has already developed good mindfulness. Otherwise, what was meant to foster meditation may become a very unprofitable time perhaps accompanied by the seeming intensification of the mental defilements.

As to the other sort of meditation practice which is performed in daily life, though much might be written, the following few words may serve as a guide. First, one should not deceive oneself or to others that one's daily life is one's meditation, unless of course one has already good concentration. Only the real adept, often one who has sat for many years keeping the monastic discipline, can really perceive ordinary life as meditation and such a one would be most unlikely to tell others of this fact. Refusing to allow pride and opportunity to distort the real state of mental affairs, one should take stock with fairness and admit one's limitation. This is already a great step forward. The person who thinks that Arahantship has already been attained has blocked off very effectively all real progress, while the honest person has at least the wisdom to be humble.

> *Conceiving so his foolishness*
> *the fool is thereby wise,*

> *While 'fool' is called-that fool*
> *conceited that he's wise.*
>
> Dhammapada 63

Much may be accomplished with mindfulness but without it there is no hope for meditation in daily life. How are quite ordinary events capable of being made into meditation? By mindfulness which to begin with may be defined as "awareness of the present work in hand" At first, great effort has to be made in order to remain mindful of what one is supposed to be doing, nor can one pretend that such mindfulness is pleasant always. To escape from dull and unliked work and situations, we tend to turn to fantasy worlds—the escape from the present, hopes and fears which are the escape to the future, or else to memories which are the escape into the past. But for one who is really interested in self-understanding none of these courses are very rewarding since they are compounded of delusion with various other ingredients such as fear, craving or unknowing. During the practice of strict meditation, mindfulness may follow all the wanderings of the mind, but in daily life it is better that the mind should be constantly returned to the job in hand. One should not 'send' one's mind anywhere, neither to a dream world, nor to the past, nor to the future. Buddhist teachers have compared these periods of time to

> *"The past is like a dream,*
> *The future as a mirage seems,*
> *While as the present—clouds."*

Such similes may be useful as the mind darts about between dreams, mirages and clouds, all insubstantial, though the ever-changing present, so like the clouds in the sky, is the only aspect of time compared to things of greater reality. One may also consider meditation as the exercise of mindfulness which keeps the mind 'inside' this body, that is, always focused upon some aspect of it. Of course only the most sincere meditator who sees advantage in this as greater than any pleasure offered by the world is likely to practise in this way since it cuts off not only interest in outer objects but also the toying with pleasant or intriguing ideas.

Indeed with work that is really uninteresting, the way of mindfulness is the only way to convert one's day into something worthwhile. Days pass and bring us nearer to death and an unknown rebirth while it is now that one has chance to practise Dhamma. Instead of reacting with aversion or deluded fantasies towards what one does not like, or in other situations indulging one's greed, the Way of Mindfulness is the practice transcending these ancient patterns of reaction. There is no need to be ruled either by greed or by aversion or to be dominated by delusion though only mindfulness shows the way beyond them.

Constantly bringing the mind back and disengaging it from tangles is the basic practice in everyday life. It is also wise to take advantage of those odd times during work when one is waiting for something to do, to meet someone, for a bus or train or any time when one is alone for a few minutes. Instead of turning to newspaper for distraction, to the wireless or to another person for gossip, it is more profitable to 'retire inside' oneself. Disengaging attention from exterior subjects, take up mindfulness of breathing or the repetition of some phrase of Dhamma or significant word such as 'Buddho', or 'Araham,' doing this until one has again to attend to work. Going inwards as often as possible will be found very useful, strengthening one's sitting practice just as the latter in turn strengthens the ability to turn within.

Mindfulness of breathing is especially good as a concentration method for use during travel and during the times when one is restlessly expecting a bus or train. Why be agitated or impatient? A little mindful breathing is just the practice for these moments since it calms the feverish workings of the mind and the restless movements of the body. One does not have to stare aimlessly out of windows while travelling! Why be a slave of the 'eye-dominant' when a little useful practice could take its place? One does not have to listen to the idle chatter of others so why be a slave to the 'ear-dominant'? One cannot shut one's ears but everyone can withdraw attention to some extent while practising mindfulness.

It is mindfulness also which helps to bring into focus counteractive contemplations. Lust for instance, is soon dissipated by thoughts of a decaying corpse. The looks which are bestowed on pretty girls or handsome men seem ridiculous when it is thought that old ladies and equally ancient men never attract such desire-filled attention. Only when one sees how lust burns up that one who indulges in it, only then does it seem worth relinquishing.

Similarly, gluttony even in a mild form can be demolished by contemplating the bodily processes connected with food. Chewed food looks a good deal less palatable than when the same stuff was nicely laid out on plates before mixing with spittle. Vomit is just the same substances in the process of change but does not readily arouse greed. Excrement even if placed on the finest gold plate fails to become attractive—yet this is the remnants of the food so eagerly gorged. By the time that one has contemplated food in these three stages, greed has quite disappeared and one may take food just as a medicine to preserve the body.

Mindfulness is also responsible for becoming sufficiently aware in a moment of anger to turn the mind to other subjects or persons. It is mindfulness that warns one of an approaching situation where anger may arise and makes it possible to turn aside and dwell in equanimity, or where the Divine Abidings are well-developed, in Loving-kindness.

When envy rears its ugly head, mindfulness gives one presence of mind to know 'envy has arisen', and if efforts to arouse gladness-with-others'-Joy fail, it is mindfulness that helps one dwell in equanimity, or if all else fails, helps turn attention to other objects.

The Buddha has truly said, "Mindfulness I declare, is everywhere of use." The social implications of meditation should be obvious from the above. Those who have the strange delusion that Buddhism

is a religion of meditative isolation offering society no social benefits should understand that a Buddhist believes society can only be
changed for the better and with some degree of permanence, by
starting work on oneself. Buddhist ideals of society are expressed in
a number of important discourses addressed by the Buddha to
laypeople and in them the development of the individual is always
stressed as a very necessary factor. The advantages of a society in
which there are a large number of those dwelling at peace with
themselves need hardly be stressed. The development of wisdom
and compassion by one person has its effect in leavening the
materialistic dough around. The Buddhist call is therefore **first** to
gain peace in one's own heart when will **follow** quite naturally, peace
in the world. Trying to obtain peace the other way round will never
be practical nor produce a lasting peace for the Roots of Greed,
Aversion and Delusion have still a firm grip on the hearts of people.
Impractical? Yes, but only for those who do not practise. Those
who take up the cultivation of mindfulness find out for themselves
how it helps to solve life's problems.

THE DIVINE ABIDINGS

The Way to Nibbana leads through what are called the Divine
Abidings* which train the deep-rooted emotions from being
unwholesome into the wholesome Way of Dhamma. It has been
emphasized above that the aim of oneself as of all beings, is to gain
happiness-producing conditions. Therefore one must act in such a
way that happiness will result from one's actions. One should, in
this case, treat others as they would wish to be treated, for every
living being is dear to itself and wishes its own welfare and happiness.
One cannot expect to have an isolated happiness arising from no
cause or from itself, nor can happiness be expected if one maltreats
other beings, human or otherwise. Every being desires life and is
afraid of death, this is as true of ourselves as of other creatures.

Only if one constantly leads an upright and compassionate life is one really dear to oneself, for then one does actions which are of great profit, of great happiness. Other people although they think that they are dear to themselves are really their own worst enemies, for they go about doing to themselves what only an enemy would wish for them. One should wish then "May I be able to protect my own happiness."

Good conduct then, depends on a well-trained mind which has gradually been freed from the clutches of Greed, Aversion and Delusion. To hold one's neighbour as dear as one should truly hold oneself is said with ease but with difficulty done. The teaching to be employed is that of the Divine Abidings of which there are four states: Loving-kindness,* Compassion,* Gladness* and Equanimity.*

These, especially the first, are very popular meditations in Buddhist countries and what follows is a short explanation of each one. Loving-kindness is an unselfish love which can be extended to everyone. This becomes easy once one has gained the absorbed concentrations when the quality of Loving-kindness becomes an integral part of one's character. In the usual way of things, people only 'love' the few people to whom they are specially attached by ties of family, etc. Such is love with sensual attachment, a limited love and those outside that love are either ignored (regarded with indifference = delusion), or disliked (regarded as enemies = aversion). Sensual love then is not only linked to attachment (= greed) but also to aversion and delusion so that the person who is content with this love, pays a heavy price for it. A love without attachment is scarcely conceivable to many people but such love is much superior to the attached kind; being without attachment it can become infinite and need not be confined to this or that group of beings. As it can be made infinite, leaving none outside it, so there is no question of the Three roots of Evil being linked with it.[29]

29. There exist, in some quarters, the peculiar notion that Buddhism is a 'coldly rational system.' To deal with these concepts: 'cold' means unsympathetic, which a true Buddhist

Loving-kindness can be developed gradually in one's meditation period every day, but if it is really effective it must show in one's daily life. It makes life easier by turning persons whom one formerly disliked or hated into, at the beginning, those whom one disregards, and then as one's practice becomes stronger, into objects for the arising of Loving-kindness. It is the Buddha's medicine for the disease of hatred and dislike. The old commentators warn one that it has two enemies: the 'near' one is sensual attachment while the 'far' enemy to its development is aversion. In the development of loving-kindness one must beware of these two.

Compassion is taking note of the sufferings of other beings in the world. It overcomes callous indifference to the plight of suffering beings, human or otherwise. It must be reflected in one's life by a willingness to go out of one's way to give aid where possible and to help those in distress. It has the advantage of reducing one's selfishness by understanding others' sorrows. It is the Buddha's medicine for cruelty, for how can one harm others when one has seen how much they suffer already? It has also two enemies: the 'near' one is mere grief, while its 'far' enemy is cruelty.

Gladness is to rejoice with others over their successes, gains and happiness. It overcomes the grudging attitude to others and the jealousy which may arise on hearing of others' joy. It must show in one's life as a spontaneous joy at the very time when one learns that other people have some gain or other, material or immaterial. It has the advantage of making one open-hearted towards others and does away with secretiveness. A person who develops gladness attracts many devoted friends and with them and others lives in harmony.

---

never is from the practice of Loving-kindness. 'Rational' here seems to imply that Buddhism can all be understood with the ordinary powers of reason whereas it has been pointed out that true understanding comes only with Insight when vast areas of mind open up, areas quite unknown by 'reason'. The parts of mind known normally are as a raindrop compared to the oceans. 'System' implies that human experience in all its richness and complexity can be compressed into a rigid psychological pattern and that human beings are like giant switchboards with just so many circuits.

It is the Buddha's medicine for envy which it can inhibit completely. The two enemies of gladness are the merely personal happiness of reflection on one's own gains—this is the 'near' enemy, while the 'far' one is aversion to or boredom with this gladness.

Equanimity is to be developed to deal with situations where one should admit that it is beyond one's powers to do anything. It overcomes worry and useless distraction over affairs which either do not concern one or else cannot be changed by oneself. It is reflected in one's life by an ability to meet difficult situations with tranquillity and undisturbed power of mind. The advantage to be seen in its development is that it makes one's life more simple by disengaging one from useless activity. It is the Buddha's medicine for distraction and worry, and its enemies are mere indifference, the 'near' one, while greed and its partner aversion which involve one un-wholesomely in so many affairs, are its 'far' enemies. The mind well-practised in these four virtues and then well-trained by their use in daily life, has already gained very much.

Three Perfections should also be outlined here as they too have an intimate bearing on the practice of Meditation.

PATIENCE AND ITS PERFECTION

This is an excellent quality much praised in Buddhist scriptures. It can only be developed easily if restlessness and aversion have already been subdued in the mind, as is done by meditation practice. Impatience which has the tendency to make one rush around and thus miss many good chances, results from the inability to sit still and let things sort themselves out, which sometimes they may do without one's meddling. The patient person has many a fruit fall into their lap which the go-getter misses. One of them is quiet mind, for impatience churns the mind up and brings with it the familiar anxiety-diseases of the modern business world. Patience quietly endures—it is this quality which makes it so valuable in mental training and particularly in meditation. It is no good expecting instant enlightenment after five minutes practice. Coffee may be instant but meditation is not and only harm will come of trying to hurry it up. For ages the rubbish has accumulated, an enormous pile of mental refuse and so when one comes along at first with a very tiny teaspoon and starts removing it, how fast can one expect it to disappear? Patience is the answer and determined energy to go with it. Patient meditators really get results of lasting value, the seeker after 'quick methods' or 'sudden enlightenment' are doomed by their own attitude to long disappointment.

Indeed, it must soon become apparent to anyone investigating the Dhamma that these teachings are not for the impatient. A Buddhist views the present life as a little span perhaps of eighty years or so, and the last one so far of many such lives. Bearing this in mind, one determines to do as much in this life for the attainment of Enlightenment as possible but one does not over-estimate one's capabilities and just quietly and patiently gets on with living the dhamma from day to day. Rushing headlong at Enlightenment (or what one thinks it is) like a bull in a china shop, is not likely to get one very far, unless one is a very exceptional character who can take such treatment and is devoted to a very skilful master of meditation.

With patience one will not bruise oneself but go carefully step by step along the Way. We learn that the Bodhisatta was well aware of this and that he cultured his mind with this Perfection so that it was not disturbed by any of the untoward occurrences common in this world. He decided that he would be patient with exterior conditions—not be upset when the sun was too hot or the weather too cold; not be agitated by other beings which attacked his body, such as bugs and mosquitoes. Neither would he be disturbed when people uttered harsh words, lies or abuse about him, either to his face or behind his back. His patience was not even broken when his body was subjected to torment, blows, sticks and stones, tortures and even death itself he would endure steadily, so unflinching was his patience. Buddhist monks and nuns are advised to practise in the same way.

In Buddhist tradition, the Perfection of Patience is rather better known than some of the others. This is because a quite outstanding Birth Story illustrates it. The Khantivadi (The Teacher of Patience) Birth Story should be read many times and made the object of deep and frequent reflections. Only an exceptionally noble person, in this case Gotama in a previous life when he was called the Patience teaching Sage, can gently exhort a drunk and raging monarch who out of his jealous anger is slowly cutting that person's body to pieces. Such nobility did the Bodhisatta have, and such nobility, steadfast endurance and gentleness is required of all who would try to reach the goal of Enlightenment.

ENERGY AND ITS PERFECTION

Just as Enlightenment is inconceivable unless a person has patience, so it is not attainable without effort being made. The Dhamma never encourages the doctrine of fatalism and true Buddhists never think of events as being rigidly predetermined. Such fatalism is combatted by mindfulness and by energy itself. This Perfection is the counterpart of the previous one and balanced by practice they ensure that a person neither passively accepts what should be combatted nor rushes around to the disturbance of self and others.[30]

30. By way of warning it may be mentioned here that in the Buddhist world can be found a number of 'methods' which seem to promise the riches of Dhamma all in no time. One hears such remarks as "What's the use of books and study!" Or even, "The development of calm is a waste of time! One should only develop "insight." Such lop-sided approaches do not reflect the wisdom of the Buddha who taught time and again the necessity of a balanced development of mind. Books and their study are useful to some people who wish to gain a good background knowledge of what Lord Buddha really said, before taking up more intensive practice. As for the other assertion, no real insight (only delusive ideas) will arise for the person whose mind has no experience of calm. Such 'views' as these which are usually based on some peculiar experience of those 'teachers' who originate them, are apt to mislead many since the craving for quick results coupled with

One should apply oneself steadily to whatever task one has in hand and coming to the end of it, not feel tired at all but straightaway take up a new objective.

It is interesting in this respect that tiredness is of two kinds: that relating to physical exhaustion and the other kind which is mentally induced and involves the unwholesome factors of sloth and torpor. While the former is of course, unavoidable, the latter only occurs when the Unwholesome Root of Delusion (or dullness) becomes predominant in the mind. This happens when there is a situation which is unpleasant, unwanted, and from which 'I' want to escape. People complain that they become much more tired sitting in meditation than they do when say, they do a bit of light reading. When one's self feels threatened by a self-revealing event, then it throws up a dense fog of torpor from the Root of Delusion. On the other hand, many who have practised much meditation remark that they do not have to sleep so long as they did formerly, while Energy when it becomes a Perfection as practised by the Bodhisatta, is quite natural and unforced.

This Perfection is illustrated by the story of the caravan-leader who saved the merchants, men and animals entrusted to his care by vigorous action. When others would have given themselves up to death since the caravan had taken a wrong course in the desert and all supplies were exhausted, their leader forced one of them to dig for water and found it. In this way, in a previous life did Gotama as the caravan-leader make efforts not only for his own life but also for the welfare of others. Monks are also referred to as 'caravan-leaders' in several places in Pali scriptures showing that it is not only the Buddha or a Bodhisatta who is able to guide others. If we deal energetically with our own training then we too have energy for the advancement of others. Many other stories like the above could be

the dislike of the necessary hard work, are easily stirred up. There must be patience to accept that the conditions required for success of meditation (as outlined here) have to be fulfilled and the only result of failing to do so is straying off the Way.

found in Buddhist works show how necessary is energy, from which spring persistence and determination, for the seeing of the truly real, Nibbana.

COLLECTEDNESS AND ITS PERFECTION

Bearing in mind the meaning of this word we may now examine what perfect collectedness is. What especially marks off the good Buddhist's practice from that of an ordinary meditator (in any religion), is that the latter will most likely become firmly attached to the delights occurring in the upper reaches of the Sensual Realm or to the pure joys of the Realm of Form and as a result, come to birth in one of those heaven states. If one gets trapped in one of these bourns where pleasures and joys are great and sufferings little, then it is unlikely that one will be able to generate the energy necessary for the Perfection of Wisdom. Therefore, the good meditator tries to become proficient in the concentrations (so that they can be entered when and which of them one likes, remain absorbed in them for as long as one likes, and emerge when one likes), while at the same time cultivating a non-attachment to them.

The heights of this Perfection are to be seen in penetration to the Truth of the Three Marks of Existence, when the powerful collected mind is used for examination of mind and body, the constituents of 'self.' In this way one comes to know the impermanence of the Five Groups: Body, Feeling, Memory/Recognition, Mental Formations, and Consciousness; that these impermanent, unstable and unreliable groups are therefore dukkha; and that of these groups tied up with dukkha and deteriorating all the time it is not possible to say: "This is mine, this am I, this is my self." In this way insight is applied to reach Enlightenment.

A story which brings out the meaning of this Perfection is told of Kuddalamuni's life. His name means the Mattock-sage, so called because of the difficulty he experienced in freeing himself from attachment to his mattock. Several times leaving his house with intent to meditate in the forest, he was dragged back by the memory of his mattock and his old occupation of farming. One day reflecting on the inconstancy with which he pursued meditation, he took his mattock and whirling it round his head, sent it spinning into the depths of the nearby Ganges. Having done this, he burst out, "I have conquered!" The local rajah who was passing that way with his army heard this (and kings on the whole do not like to hear of others who have conquered!) and inquired what it was that this farmer had conquered. The sage replied by relating his experience. The rajah and many others were much impressed by his reply and some followed him to take up a meditative life in the forest after which we are told, all passed away to experience life in the Realm of Subtle Form. The Mattock-sage who was none other than Gotama in a past life, exhibited even then another aspect of the Perfection of Meditation: the ability to train others in meditation after gaining proficiency in it himself.

Finally, in this section we may add brief notes on three other good qualities which are both useful for meditation and are augmented by its practice.

Contentment* is a brightly shining star in the constellation of wholesome qualities. This exists on many levels, from animal up to that of Perfect Enlightenment. We are concerned not with the lowest, but the Buddhist type of contentment. With enough of the necessities of life, one's mind will only be distracted if many desires crowd in as well. More and more things possessed actually do not satisfy, they are a cause for future dissatisfaction. With many things one has to have many more things, and more, and more. This is the opposite of contentment, but must not be thought of as an excuse for laziness which all the Buddha's Teachings condemn. The simple life, on the other hand, is not lived happily merely by being frugally economic, it comes of an inward peace, of thoughts not outward straying after this or that thing, but contented to stay at home in the heart. It does not exclude dynamic growth in Dhamma which is truly much easier with contentment than without it.

Then there is **gratitude**. The Pali words for this are a pair usually found together: gratitude and requiting others.* Through the practice of meditation, one does become more aware of the help and kindness of others, and even becomes grateful for harsh words when these spur one on to practice. One's gratitude grows towards one's Dhamma-teacher, for parents and teachers who have given so much time and energy to oneself, and to friends as well who may have helped with the living of a good Dhamma-life. And one is not only grateful to them in one's heart but one wishes to benefit them in turn, to requite their kindness. The Buddha says that it is the mark of the wise person to be grateful and requite others, but of the fool ingratitude is the mark.

Finally, **humility*** should be mentioned here. This quality cannot be simulated To pretend or even to believe that one is humble is merely false humility, otherwise pride dressed up differently. Humility is not a quality by which the world sets very much store, especially these days. The 'successful' person is apparently the one who goes out and wrests fortune from the world and then exhibits it for all to see. But Buddhist eyes may look further than this little life and in a longer perspective it will appear that humility is indeed the winner. Success in worldly matters is fleeting (though worthwhile when devoted to others' benefit), whereas coming to understand oneself has an incalculably greater effect. Humility is necessary, for instance, in approaching a religious tradition so venerable as the Buddhist one. Before one starts condemning this or that, pause a moment, does one understand everything connected with those matters? Perhaps, after all it is one's own mind which is at fault? It is needed again if one goes to a teacher to learn, say, meditation. No humility means the presence of pride, this leading to egocentric rigidity. Where this is present, there is no hope of learning for which flexibility is required. Last but not least, humility is needed when presenting one's own opinions or ideas. They may be good, but if they relate to Dhamma, one must always remember that they spring from a mind still imperfect.

DANGERS IN MIND-TRAINING

While the number of ways a meditator may go astray are legion, the few mentioned below deserve special attention due to their common occurrence. First, a danger that cannot be stressed enough is the lack of right motivation for the practice of meditation. In the Eightfold Path's wisdom section, after Right Understanding, which is at first intellectual, come Right Intention. This emphasizes that the emotional roots underlying practice of the Way must be wholesome ones: Those connected with generosity and renunciation (non-greed), loving-kindness (non-aversion) and compassion (non-violence) are mentioned. If one approaches Buddhist meditation with neither Right Understanding regarding dukkha and its cessation, nor with Right Intention, then one's meditation is liable to go seriously astray.

There have, for instance, been those who took up meditation as a way to invest themselves with power so that they could easily sway or hypnotize disciples. Others have seen it as a quick way to gain both disciples and riches. Fame may also be an unworthy motive. All these, which are just playing with meditation, may easily lead the unwary into illness and sometimes, mental unbalance. there is nothing worse in meditation where a person's own sure experience is of paramount importance, than a half-baked disciple who sets himself up as a master.

This obviously leads on to a further danger—that of pride, of which there are several forms. One such is the pride of the person who has seen manifestations of light during meditation and supposes this to be the sign preceding absorbed concentration. Then there is the pride of one who touches on an absorbed concentration if only for an instant and as a result assumes that Arahantship has been attained. This can be a very powerful factor in convincing oneself if not others. Quite ordinary people who take up meditation may beware of the common 'holier-than-thou' attitudes: "I make an effort, you..." or, "I meditate every day, you..." Pride is a great obstacle to any progress and while it is only a Buddha or Arahant who is rid of it, everyone should have mindfulness to check it.

Related to this is the danger for the person who always looks for so-called progress. One is sure that one is making 'progress' because in meditation one sees lights, hears sounds or feels strange sensations. One becomes more and more fascinated by these as time goes by and gradually forgets that one started with the aspiration to find the Way to Enlightenment. One's 'meditation' then degenerates into visions and strange happenings leading into realms of occultism and magic. There is no surer way for a meditator to become entangled than this way. Fascinating though all such manifestations may be, they should be rigorously cut down by resorting to bare attention, never permitting discursive thought regarding them and thus avoiding these distractions.

Another danger is trying to meditate while still too emotionally insecure, unbalanced or immature. An understanding of the value of merit will come in useful here. As merit purifies the mind, it will be an excellent basis for meditation and both the ease with which concentrations are gained and the ease with which insight arises are to some extent dependent upon merit. **Merit**, one should always remember, **opens doors everywhere**. it makes possible, it makes opportunities. To have a mind at all times set upon practising Dhamma, is to have one that develops concentrations and insight easily.

If follows that to try to practise meditation while all the time retaining one's old cravings, likes and dislikes, is to say the least, making one's path difficult, if not dangerous. Meditation implies renunciation and no practice will be successful unless one is at least prepared to make efforts to restrain greed and aversion, check lust and understand when delusion is clouding the heart. How far one carries renunciation and whether this involves outward changes (such as becoming a monk or nun), depends much on the individual but one thing is sure: inward renunciation, an attitude of giving-up with regard to both unwholesome mental events and bodily indulgence, is absolutely essential.

Often connected with the above dangers is another, to be seen in cases where a person suddenly has an opportunity to undertake a long period of meditation practice. One sits down with the firm resolve, "Now I shall meditate" but though one's energy is ever so great and though one sits and sits and walks and walks, still one's mind is disturbed and without peace. It may well be that one's own strong effort has much to do with the distractions. Moreover, one has to learn that it is necessary to meditate knowing the limitations of character. Just as any other worker who knows the limits of bodily strength and is careful not to overwork so is the able meditator careful. With mindfulness one should know the extremes of laziness and strain to be avoided.

It is through straining or forcing meditation practice that many emotionally disturbed states arise. Sudden bursts of intense anger all over insignificant trifles. fierce cravings and lusts, strange delusions and even more peculiar fantasies can all be produced from unwisely arduous practice.

With all these dangers it is a skilled teacher who is most necessary to give advice so that these and other wrong turnings are avoided and one keeps straight along the Way to Nibbana. Those who are without a teacher should proceed with the utmost caution making sure that their development of mindfulness is very good indeed. If they are mindful and see that despite their efforts, their meditation practice is making no real difference to their lives in terms of greater internal peace, or externally in relation to others, then it should be apparent that something is wrong. Meditation may be laid aside for some time while making efforts to contact a genuine source of information, preferably a living meditation teacher.

For further details on meditation there are also many books to consult, some of them good, while in Thailand there is the living tradition which may be contacted if one is interested. If the section in this book upon Practice has been shorter than that on Belief, this is not because the latter is more prominent in the Dhamma than the former. Practices can only be known by practising! The best way to know what water is like is not gotten at through words! One will find out much better by splashing about in it! If one wants Enlightenment, one has to have enough interest to do the practice. Even though ten thousand books ten times this size might hold all the practical details, what would be the use of them without the accompanying practice?

The three sections which have now been considered, Mundane Wisdom, Virtue and Collectedness are factors which are not peculiar to the Dhamma taught by the Buddha as they are found in all good Teachings in varying proportions. But not all religious teachings have a fully developed Wisdom-tradition which begins to grow with Virtue, develops with practice of mind-culture, and blossoms fully with realization.

PART III

WHAT DO BUDDHISTS REALIZE?

As a result of practice, what was at first believed out of respect for the Wisdom of the Buddha, is finally seen as the Truth within one's mind and body so that one is "One-Who-Knows, One-Who-Sees,"* no longer having faith. To complete our enquiry therefore, some effort should be made to set down a few words upon.

4. SUPERMUNDANE WISDOM*

LIMITATIONS OF WORDS

To begin with we should be aware of the weaknesses of language when it is used for the supermundane for which it was never intended and has no words to describe anyway. Anyone reading the Buddha's Discourses will notice that much is said of this world, not only because it is useful for ordinary people but because there are words to describe it. Less is said of the heavens of Sense-desire although the superlatives of adjectives describing earthly delights will do. The Realms of Subtle from are only described, if indeed this is the right word for such brief formulae, by a few sentences relating which mental-emotional factors are present at the levels of absorbed concentrations corresponding to them. Words are already insufficient! Reaching the Formless Realms, words are useless since they usually describe 'things' (physical and mental)—which these realms are far beyond. Each one is therefore labeled with only one compound Pali word. But this is all the world of birth-and-death, and all of it may to some extent be named, conceptualized and reasoned about. The Noble Ones and particularly the Arahants, have so to speak, jumped off this whirling roundabout and discovered Nibbana, or the Deathless. In 'describing' this, words are only useful if used with great care.

It is a feature of ordinary people to use words carelessly due to the belief that the things described by them are real entities which exist permanently. It would be truer to say that 'words use the worlding' rather than the reverse. The deluded mind has formed words and put them together as language; the deluded mind then uses them mistaking the changing and impermanent events of certain continuities (the substance of my body is all the time changing but it remains a body) for permanent realities. Language and lack of insight (the presence of delusion) camouflage the real world and condition us to see it through a haze of misconceptions.

RELATIVE AND ULTIMATE TRUTH

Buddhist psychology does not deny the **relative** validity of the concept of a person, nor the **relative** existence of being. It does not deny that Mr. Smith or Ms. Jones exist but it does point out that they only have continuity dependent on certain factors. Dependently they are born, dependently they exist and dependently they die. Dependently originated 'persons' described by using words, are 'true'—relatively true. Thus Buddhist thought points out Relative Truth* and its whole purpose is to help people recognize this and then through Collectedness and Insight ensure that they never again mistake it for reality. The Buddha **used** words and concepts, and therefore Relative Truth, but he was not confused thereby; whereas ordinary people like ourselves let the words turn us round.

Ultimate Truth* is the direct seeing of impermanence, dukkha and no-self and hence of Nibbana, or the experience of the Void, which is to be gained after insight into the nature of the Five Groups. It is the Truth which comes with Freedom from all bondages. It is not bound up with the processes of conceptual thought but has gone completely beyond them. It is not related to anything known by the senses (and mind) and therefore strictly indescribable. One way of defining it is by negative statements since with these the mind has less chance of grasping after concepts. Consider some famous words of the Buddha: "O monks, there is that sphere where there is no earth, no water, no fire and no air, nor the sphere of infinite space, nor the sphere of infinite consciousness, nor the sphere of no-thingness, nor the sphere of neither-perception-non-perception; neither this world, nor another world and neither the sun nor the moon. I call that neither a coming nor a going, nor existence, nor passing away, nor uprising, unsupported, unmoving, devoid of object—that indeed is the end of dukkha..."

SUPERMUNDANE WISDOM AND ITS PERFECTION

'The end of dukkha' spoken of by the Buddha is the third of the Four Noble Truths. He tells us that this Truth "should be realized" and that he "has realized" it. The Third Noble Truth, the Truth of Cessation, is another way of saying Nibbana but to see how this may be discovered, a brief survey of Dependent Origination will be useful.

Dependent Origination is the most complex formulation of the Four Noble Truths and cannot be treated adequately here. In this book, it is illustrated by the twelve links around the outside of the Wheel of Birth and Death. What is said here will link up various aspects of Dhamma outlined elsewhere in this book.

The sequence of dependent arising extends from causes in past lives to results in the present one and from causes made in the present which will bring results in future lives.

The past causes are first, unknowing. This is an ignorance of the Four Noble Truths, although the first two Truths are always seen quite easily in our lives. As in the past we had this unknowing (the blind old woman leaning on a stick), so we came to make kamma, wholesome and unwholesome. This past kamma-making may be called volitional activities. So we get the first link **unknowing conditioning volition** (the potter making pots).

From the past we come now to the present life. Those past volitions or kammas become the objects for rebirth consciousness, so the next link is formed: **volition conditioning (relinking) consciousness.** This relinking (or rebirth) consciousness (shown by a monkey jumping from one tree to another) is the resultant or fruit of the past kammas and it drags along with it a lot of other kamma which thus gets the chance to bear fruit.

This can be seen in the third connection: **consciousness conditioning mind-body** (the latter a boat punted by mind with body as passenger). According to the sort of relinking consciousness, whether it is associated with human birth, animal, ghost... so will be the production of mind and body. In some cases other physical factors must assist in the production of the latter, as in the case of those born in wombs or from eggs.

Mind-body conditioning the sixfold sense-sphere (mind is the sixth). Having established the conditions for a certain type of mind and body, the senses associated with such an organism will come into existence dependent (these senses are shown by a house with six windows).

When the sixfold sense-sphere is established there is sure to be contact between sense, object and sense-consciousness. Thus we have the next connection: **the sixfold consciousness conditioning contact** (a loving man and woman). Note here what has been said of the relativity of perception in the section on Levels and Perceptions.

Contact conditioning feeling is the next connection. When we experience contact through eye, ear, nose, tongue, body and mind, the three feelings arise dependently according to what sort of contact it has been. (All feelings are dukkha in ultimate truth, hence a man with arrows piercing his eyes).

The three feelings are painful (dukkha), pleasant and neutral ones, When they have been experienced we decide to do something about them. From consciousness round to feelings there has been a succession of the fruits of kamma but at this point we begin to make new kamma in the present life to bring results in future. The connection here is **feeling conditioning craving**. Mindfulness of feelings can at this point check the onward rush of this wheel.

Craving (shown as a thirsty drunken man) is for sense-pleasures, for continued existence, or for an end of existence. When craving has its way, dependent upon it will arise clinging or grasping for the five groups comprising oneself. So this connection is **craving conditioning grasping**, (the latter is represented by a person reaching for fruit).

Grasping conditioning becoming is the next connection. Becoming (depicted as a pregnant woman) means becoming other all the time, constant change influenced by grasping. At the end of life one wishes to become human, a god, and so on. With the right sort of kamma this can be achieved.

But in the process of becoming there is plenty of dukkha to be suffered in various ways. So now one makes for oneself the dukkha to be felt in the future, this connection being: **Becoming conditioning birth**. Even birth in the heavenly realms is still dukkha because of the impermanence of all life. (Birth is illustrated by a woman in childbirth).

And it is certain that all birth will end in aging and dying (see the illustration of an old man and a corpse) so the last connection is **birth conditioning old age and death**.

This is called "the arising of this whole mass of dukkha" and was seen by the Buddha at the time of his Enlightenment. This is the Second Noble Truth of the Arising of Dukkha, the way to more birth and death and all the troubles in between. But he saw also the

way out of this mess which is the Third Noble Truth of Cessation.
The text of the way out reads like this:

"This unknowing, through its entire ceasing, volition ceases

volition ceasing	consciousness ceases
consciousness ceasing	mind-body ceases
mine-body ceasing	sixfold sense-sphere ceases
sixfold sense-sphere ceasing	contact ceases
contact ceasing	feeling ceases
feeling ceasing	craving ceases
craving ceasing	grasping ceases
grasping ceasing	becoming ceases
becoming ceasing	birth ceases
birth ceasing	old-age and death: sorrow,

lamentation, pain, grief and despair cease. Thus is the ceasing of
this whole mass of dukkha."

All these factors are called dhammas and at the end of this book
there is a verse, the third line of which states:
"When dhammas for that one have been destroyed…"
This refers to this process of cessation. The timid person will be
afraid that all this cessation means annihilation. But it means really
annihilation of Greed, Aversion and Delusion, of Ignorance and
Craving. The ordinary person may be afraid of this because most of
'oneself' is reared upon the sinking sands of these defilements. The
wise person is not afraid for s/he relies upon the bedrock of
Dhamma.

WHOLESOME MEANS AND ITS PERFECTION

The possession of means, more or less wholesome, by an unenlightened person rather depends on merits of which intelligence
is an aspect, for this, in a balanced individual, may promote the
desire to help others. Even at the embryonic stage of this perfection

the link with wisdom can be seen though these two aspects of Enlightenment remain quite isolated due to egocentricity and the Roots of Unwholesomeness. Only when the latter have been up-rooted and Wisdom becomes the basis for true knowledge of oneself and the world, only then can great Compassion arise. While Wisdom sees no beings to save, analysis into events (dhammas) and the resolution of those into the Void having dissolved everyone of them, Compassion vows to help them all, taking note of all the various ills from which beings suffer. Wisdom and Compassion while fragmented in the ordinary person, are the two banks of the same stream of Enlightenment in a Buddha or an Arahant.

Wholesome Means are the natural expression of Compassion. If compassion was only the thinking of 'compassionate' thoughts, the Buddha and the Arahants would have dwelt in lifelong silence and solitude. They did not do this! Compassion, as noted under the section of Divine Abidings, has to show in one's life by com-passionate action. There is no more compassionate action than the showing of Dhamma to those who wish to see, or to those who could see but have had no chance to do so. The lives of the En-lightened One illustrates this Perfection at its highest development. The Buddha taught just the right level of Dhamma to those who came to him. To the brahmins who wanted to be born into a Brahma-world, he showed the Path of practice which would lead them there. To those who aspired to the lower heavens of desire, he satisfied them by explaining the course leading to that rebirth. To those concerned with this life and happiness here and now, to them he showed how this might be obtained. To the herdsman he spoke Dhamma in terms of cattle while to the farmer he pointed out that the fruit reaped by himself was the Fruit of Deathlessness (Nibbana). Such stories in the Dhammapada Commentary as that of the Weaver's daughter, or the famous tale of Kisa Gotami and her dead child—in these are seen the Perfection of Wholesome Means. By means of this Perfection the Buddha was able to satisfy the haughtiest of warrior princes, the most deeply learned pundits from among the brahmins, as easily as he could show the Way to the poor and uneducated, the scavengers and outcasts—for Enlightenment provides a wholesome means for every occasion.

Nor was this Perfection grown up suddenly in one life. We read that the Bodhisatta when taking birth as a deer called Nandiya, saved his old and blind parents whom he lovingly supported, from the hunters by use of a wholesome means. Whether we too are able to help others to Dhamma and to what extent we are able to do so, depends upon our compassion and that in turn upon many other factors. It is the taking up of the whole Dhamma into one's heart which changes one from being an unenlightened ordinary person to an Enlightened One.

TRUTH AND ITS PERFECTION

We make a start by observing the Fourth Precept and then by developing its counterpart, Truthfulness. After this, learning of the two levels of truth, relative and ultimate, by the practice of Dhamma we become more aware of these, seeing the provisional nature of the first and striving to penetrate the second.

At the moment of Enlightenment, as in the case of the Buddha and other Buddhist sages, there arises perfected knowledge of this ultimate Truth which we may call the Truly-so, or seeing-dhammas-as-they-really-are. There is a thread of truth joining together all stages of the Buddhist Way. After there has been the experience of Nibbana then as the Buddha has said, "Truth is one without a second."

The practice of this Perfection at a more humble stage is seen in the well-known Birth Story of Vidhurapandita who, having been captured in the forest by a cannibal, so fearlessly set about making the ordered preparations for his own death as to rouse the curiosity of his captor. The latter permitted him to return to his city for a short time as a test of his veracity and although many others less worthy than himself offered themselves to satisfy the cannibal's craving, Vidhurapandita insisted on returning as he had promised to do. The reward of his truthfulness was that the cannibal was greatly moved by his nobility, released him from his obligations and was himself converted to the practice of the five Precepts.

Such is the power of truth, that Buddhists have been accustomed to make asservations of Truth, declaring that if such and such be true, then let such and such happen. So mighty is truth's power, really the power of what is in accordance with Dhamma, that great wonders have been effected.

Viewing truth in another way, from the point of view of persons, more light may be shed on the nature of Buddhist realization in the following section.

FROM ORDINARY TO NOBLE PERSONS

The Great Teacher once classified humanity according to a fourfold scheme he said: "Here a certain person practises neither for their own benefit nor for that of another; a second practises for another's benefit but not for their own welfare; then there is the third one who practises for their own benefit but not for another's; while the fourth person practises both for their own benefit and for another's."

In this scheme we see all the spectrum of human life from the evil person who lives as enemy of self and others, right round to the Buddhist ideal of the wisdom which sees one's own benefit united with the compassion seeing the benefit of others.

First then, comes one who practises neither for their own nor for other's advantage. This is defined by saying that neither such a one makes an effort to destroy Greed, Aversion and Delusion within, nor incites others to make efforts. Content to live with the Evil Roots this person will suffer the consequences of lack of diligence. Moreover others must also suffer. A thoroughly egocentric person of this sort living only to grab what can be gotten from the world will be no blessing to anyone. While this one looks only to self, the next of the four persons goes to the other extreme, looking only to others.

One must discriminate here since there are the very rare and saintly persons who can work selflessly for the good of others (but note, they have accomplished their own good first) while the great majority of people falling under this heading will be either foolish or conceited. Later Buddhist thought emphasized the first as being the true Buddhist ideal (of the Bodhisatta) without always making it clear that in order to help others in the Way of Dhamma one must first have the wherewithal to give that help. No doubt this outlook is very noble, altruistic and so on, but often it is not very practical especially when one first puts one's feet on the Way to Enlightenment. In the case of the second type here, S/he should ask: 'Why do I want to help others?' Perhaps one's own house is in such a bad state that escape from it comes by trying to patch up others' dwellings?

First, to put one's own house in order is a cardinal rule in Buddhist training. One wastes a precious human life now by 'do-gooding' to others which is often just interfering and a waste of time instead of looking into one's own heart. In practice, teachers in the northern Buddhist traditions also exhort their Bodhisatta disciples to strive towards Enlightenment here-and-now after experiencing which they really can save all beings. Again, in practice, it has only been those who have fulfilled their own training who have been able to give help.

The third person either cannot, or does not want to aid others. Such a one cannot do so if either there is no ability to teach (such as the Hermit Buddhas and some Arahants), or if still bound to train himself and therefore not yet ready to be a teacher of others. Take, for instance, the case of monks living in forest monasteries diligently training themselves in meditation. Though they are not apparently benefitting others while training themselves, in fact many others may be inspired by their example. And in the future they may be able to give help. Dhamma can never be practised without giving benefit.

The forth type of person constitutes the Buddhist ideal of realization as a Buddha or Arahant. The latter are spoken of by the Buddha as "living for the welfare of the multitude, for the happiness of the multitude, out of compassion for the world, for the good, welfare and happiness of gods and men." The Buddha, also known by the epithet 'Arahant,' lived in just this way, arduous and compassionate for forty-five years. Moreover, in a famous and oft-quoted passage, he exhorted his first sixty disciples (all of them Arahants) in similar stirring words: "Go forth, O monks, and travel for the welfare and happiness of multitude, out of compassion for the world, for the good, welfare and happiness of gods and men. Proclaim, O monks, the glorious Dhamma teaching a life of holiness, perfect and pure." It is borne out by the lives of the Buddha's great monk-disciples that they did indeed live in this way and that their concern for others was very great. No selfishness is possible for one who has looked into what is usually called the self—the mind-body complex, and found that all ideas of self and soul are quite false. Only those who have no practical and direct knowledge of Not-self can be selfish, for they operate on egocentric assumptions. The highest service which one can render beings is to be able to show them the Way beyond the fret and turmoil of the wandering-on in birth-and-death, and this one cannot do unless one has seen it first oneself.

These four types of human beings can be compared to four stages in the growth of a lotus bud. The first type would then be represented by the tiny, hard green lotus bud bitten by fish and tortoises far down amidst the dark and muddy waters. In this simile, the second kind of person would be like the swelling lotus bud still below water but pushing its way to the surface, while the third is shown by a lotus already emerged into bright sunlight showing colour but as yet not open. The last person, whom the Buddha praises as "chief and best, foremost, highest and supreme," a Buddha or an Arahant, is compared to the graceful beauty of the fully-opened lotus, splendid in purity and of delicate, refreshing scent.

Another application of this simile would be to four persons, the first and last being the same as those described above but the middle two differing. First in this list is the 'foolish ordinary person,'* hard and immature, bereft of inward light and true happiness. The second person, as though pushing through the waters towards light, is the 'beautiful ordinary person'* intent on Dhamma-practice. Emerged from the waters of craving into the sunlight of Dhamma but not yet opened out, is the stream-attainer.* And last, "chief and best, foremost, highest and supreme" are Buddhás and Arahants who have discovered Enlightenment, blossoming as the lotus of purity, compassion and wisdom.

Let us now look at these four persons in greater detail. The ordinary person has been mentioned already, one without insight who may be of two types: either 'foolish,' given up to ignorance and craving, or 'beautiful,' one who practises some good way of Dhamma. Now, consider the first. Such a one drifts along through life variously swayed by hopes and ambitions which are coloured with Greed, Aversion and Delusion. In this wandering course there is no definite direction though bound by the bonds of unknowing to waking, travelling, working, eating, relaxation and sleeping. This person seldom considers if life could be better employed or whether there are objectives higher than this round. If having a religion, it satisfies several desires: it accords with convention, it is the tradition of the family, it involves ceremonies (in church, etc.) but does not 'poke its nose' into other affairs, serves as club for meeting business associates and other desirable people and gives a little prop of consolation occasionally—it is needed for no more than this.

As contrasted with this sombre picture, a beautiful ordinary person really practises religion and finds happiness in meritorious deeds, in keeping the Precepts and in meditation. Such a person does have a definite goal because of understanding who s/he is in this world and

where striving will get one. Though without insight, still life is both
for their own and other's benefit.

The stream-enterer, one who has gone into the Dhamma-stream
flowing to Nibbana, is the first of the Noble Ones in this Dhamma.
Their supermundane insight, the first of Nibbana, causes them to
abandon three fetters: belief that the Five Groups are 'I' or 'mine';
attachment to rites and vows taking them to be true religion; and
scepsis, the doubt that questions, 'Now was the Buddha really
Enlightened, is Dhamma the right way to Enlightenment, is there a
Sangha of Noble Ones who by practising Dhamma have found that
Enlightenment?' This scepsis cannot continue once Nibbana has
been glimpsed for one then **knows** from one's own experience: 'Yes,
the Buddha was Enlightened with Supreme Enlightenment,' and
so on.

The Arahant has broken all the fetters. These are given as ten in
number: the three above plus sensual desire, anger, desire for Subtle
Form existence, desire for Formless existence, pride, restlessness and
unknowing. While the Stream-enterer may lead the householder's
life and so may the other Noble Ones, the Arahant who is rid of
these fetters finds peace only in the Homeless life of a monk or nun.
One who would be rid of these fetters, which means to be rid of
Greed, Aversion, and Delusion must be prepared for hard work,
usually for many years. The course of training is not an easy one
and it implies for most people, going forth from home to
homelessness and staying with a Teacher of the Dhamma for an
unknown length of time in the jungle. To attain this peak of striving
in the Dhamma, adherence to the Monastic Rules, the practice of
certain allowable austerities (such as eating once a day), and earnest
application to training the wild mind with meditation, will be
necessary. But those who succeed in this quest though they may not
be very well known, are yet the very people who, being the true
Buddhists, keep this Dhamma alive and pass on the precious way to
their disciples in turn.

A poetic description of those perfected in this Dhamma may be obtained from the verses of the Dhammapada, a collection of the jewel-like sayings of the Buddha:

> *In whom is no wrong-doing*
> *by body, speech or mind,*
> *in these three ways restrained*
> *One such I say's a paragon.*

> *Whose destination is unknown*
> *to humans, spirits or to gods,*
> *pollutions faded, Arahant,*
> *One such I say's a paragon.*

> *Skilled in the Path, what's not-the-Path*
> *in wisdom deep, sagacious one,*
> *having attained the highest aim,*
> *One such I say's a paragon.*

> *In whom there are no longings found*
> *in this world or the next,*
> *longingless and free of bonds:*
> *One such I say's a paragon.*

> *Abandoned all the human bonds*
> *and gone beyond the bonds of gods,*
> *unbound one is from every bond:*
> *One such I say's a paragon.*

> *Abandoned boredom and delight,*
> *become quite cool and assetless,*
> *a hero, all-worlds-conqueror:*
> *One such I say's a paragon.*

One Noble, most excellent, heroic too,
the great sage and one who conquers all,
who's faultless, washen, one Awake,
One such I say's a paragon.

Dhammapada 391, 420, 403, 410, 417, 418, 422

NIBBANA

The word 'Nibbana' can be derived in a number of ways: **ni**, a negative particle, plus **vana**, which can be translated in various ways. It can mean 'blowing out' as of a candle-flame being snuffed out[31] (the end of the defilements' burning). Another meaning which can be derived from **vana** is 'jungle,' both the external tangle of rainforest and the internal jungle of selfish desires. Nibbana has also been explained by the famous Simile of the Burning Fire. The Buddha asked an inquirer whether he would know that a fire burning before him was burning. The inquirer said he would. Then supposing someone asked you, said the Buddha, what that fire burned dependent on. The man replied that he would say it burnt dependent on grass and sticks. But if it went out, would you know that it has gone out?—was the Buddha's next question. The reply was that he would. Then if it had gone out and someone asked you, in which direction has it gone, what would you say? The man's answer: You cannot say such a thing. It burnt while it had fuel (literally, fuel 'to cling to'). It is the same with the accomplished sage, remarked the Buddha, it is not meaningful to ask where he has gone (when the body dies). This is what words cannot describe.

Nibbana is also associated with the idea of 'becoming cool.' When the fires of passionate desires, hates and delusions in this feverish

---

31. This explanation has misled some to suppose that Nibbana is total extinction in spite of the Buddha's very explicit denials on this very subject. That which is beyond all words can scarcely be explained by the word 'annihilation' better than any other. It is ridiculous to suppose that the Buddha-dhamma could have flourished and inspired people for twenty-five centuries and in a host of countries, it had utter extinction as its goal!

life have been quenched, the heart is not agitated in any way. Free from smoldering and explosions it enjoys tranquillity or coolness.

One other very important description of Nibbana is the Other Shore. This bank of a river is seen to be dangerous with many things to arouse terror. Looking across the stream, the further bank is seen as secure, a place of beauty. The determined person gathers sticks binds them together and makes a raft which can be paddled across the river to the other bank. Reaching it one leaves the raft and goes on one's way happily. This simile tells us much about Dhamma and the goal of Nibbana. We should note the emphasis on the insecurity and unsatisfactory conditions to be found in the realm of birth-and-death. Looking from where we are to what we suppose is Nibbana, it is seen as a refuge secure, free from all afflictions. Determination is necessary to set about doing something and then sustained energy is needed in order to cross over the river—the river of constant becoming. The raft on which one goes is the Dhamma, its binding is one's Discipline (vinaya) or precepts. Also necessary in crossing a river, is to go straight across rather than drifting along, a symbol for Right View (see I, 'Suffering' and Happiness) that is needed to prevent drifting due to currents of worldly attachment, dislike, etc. Once the Other Shore is reached, the Dhamma is known in one's own heart. With the aid of the Buddha's directions one has discovered it for one self. The raft which had been so invaluable in crossing-over can now be dispensed with for then it is not the Enlightenment of Gotama the Buddha which is known second-hand through his recorded words, but one's own discovery. Such a sage goes along the way rejoicing, not being attached even to Dhamma. Even to Nibbana the sage is not attached. One has over-come completely all views and misunderstandings regarding this Nibbana or Enlightenment which block the vision of the ordinary person.

The last way in which Nibbana may be characterized is as the Unconditioned and Uncompounded. The events in the world of birth- and-death are, as noted above, conditioned or compounded by certain factors in the presence of which they arise and in the absence of which they either do not arise or else decline from existence. Nibbana stands contrasted with such evanescent and patchwork phenomena—it is not conditioned and so neither arises, nor exists due to conditions, nor passes away. This a good example of the 'negative-descriptive' way of talking about Nibbana.

Nibbana is called also in the Pali texts: "the Unconditioned, the End, the Unpolluted, the Truth, the Beyond, the Subtle, the Very-hard-to-see, the No-decay, the Stable, the Taken-leave-of, the Unindicated, the Unimpeded, the Peace, the Deathless, the Excellent, the Fortunate, the Security, the Destruction of Craving, the Wonderful, the Astonishing, the Freedom-from-harm, the Unharmed State, the Extinguished, the Harmless, the Non-attached, the Purity, the Freedom, the Done-away-with (craving), the Island, the Cave, the Shelter, the Refuge, the Ultimate Goal."

Having touched upon the heights of Nibbana and having tried to say what it is both by using positive and negative descriptions, it is now necessary to remove some misunderstands[32] about Nibbana by saying quite definitely what it is not. Notably, people have tended to conceive of the goal of religion in two ways. Most religious movements in the world have thought of the Absolute in terms of infinite existence and of the person who passes into knowledge of (or dwelling with) that Absolute as then enjoying everlasting existence (as either fusing with the Absolute,[33] living in company with it/him/her, or else some stage of partial dualism). This the extreme view of **Eternalism**. Much trouble has come about because people did not realize that their puny words which are fit for

---

32. Nibbana, the Buddhist goal has been equated with the goals of other religions. The question, is not whether they are the same but upon what authority pronouncements of 'sameness' are made. If it is upon the comparison of descriptions in different religions' books then this is a case of comparing realizations while having only book-learning. Those who have come to realize the goal of their respective religions will be unlikely to argue. The Buddha advised practice, not comparison.

33. Although Sir Edwin Arnold's "the dewdrop slips into the Shining Sea," is a good

farming, fighting and even for philosophy, will not do when one deals with an Absolute. Speculation, as the Buddha proclaimed so clearly, is useless. Either you **know**, or you do not. No amount of wrangling on theological subtleties will settle the matter. Such speculation is called False View, false because leading away from Nibbana, and false since based on Unwholesome Roots.

He was particularly concerned that people should not fall into the extreme belief of supposing that one who had gained Nibbana during life, would after death, continue to exist 'in Nibbana.' What was the danger that he saw in this? Such a **d**octrine supposes a self or soul which continues 'in Nibbana.' A self or soul is thought of as being possessed by a person, or as being one's real 'self.' Whatever is **possessed**, even such a subtle things as a soul or self, will prove a hindrance to attaining Nibbana. In Buddhist scriptures it is stressed that even Nibbana is without a 'soul-self.' This precludes both: the attainment of it by anyone who still craves for and clings to any idea of 'soul-self'; as well as ruling out any thought of Nibbana as a sort of 'overself,' 'cosmic self,' etc. So, if one would realize Nibbana which is no-self, what one calls 'oneself' must be seen as no-self. All ideas of eternalism, if analyzed, will be found to be only theories of a 'subtle-me-going-on,' in other words, one has not completely renounced theories and by way of them hangs on to an 'I-concept.'

A few teachings, religious and materialist, have presented the opposite extreme view, that of **Annihilationism**, for people's belief. Generally, it proclaims that experience of the world is begun at birth and ended at death. Such people suppose that this is the only life and stress particularly that here-and-now is the only time to get

---

poetic picture, it is not very good Dhamma. No dewdrop (a soul-entity) is there to slip into the Sea (be joined with the Absolute). This mounts to equating Nibbana with an impersonal Principle of some sort. Buddhist tradition guards against this by emphasizing that even Nibbana is devoid of any abiding entity (sabbe dhamma anatta). All dhammas (events) whether conditioned or unconditioned are not self. God, whether in personal or impersonal dress, cannot by the very nature of the Dhamma, find any place in it.

things done. Now, while in one way this is admirable as it ensures
that vital matters are not postponed, it is usually linked to a
mechanistic theory of human behavior and usually also to
materialism. Its great drawback is that it fails to inspire people for
long. It is noticeable that movements of this sort (some contem-
porary with the Buddha, as well as the ancient Indian Materialists)
do not last for long. They fail to satisfy humanity's spiritual cravings
and after some time people will look for other and more truly
religious ideals. This is already happening with Communism, the
latest materialist pseudo-religion. Eternalist views, on the other
hand, actually pander to human craving to go on and on. As they
do this they find ready support and flourish apace. Buddhism while
regarding Eternalism as a less pernicious view than annihilationism,
gives no encouragement to the former. True adherents of Dhamma
are led by their practice to give up all views whatsoever. The
Annihilation-view besides failing to inspire, may sometimes uphold
people who hedonistically enjoy today's pleasures while shrugging
their shoulders about the morrow. As theistic religions picture a
Judgement delivered by God sometime after death, so this view,
being in revolt against the God-dominated universe, may declare
that no retribution at all exists. One may do as one pleases, enjoy
oneself now, there is nothing after life. A car bumper sticker sums
up this view well, "If it feels good, do it!" If restraint is removed in
this way, by this extreme view, then Buddhist Teaching criticizes it
severely as leading to the downfall of those who follow it. Very
definitely the Buddha declared that those who said that he taught a
doctrine of annihilation were not reporting him correctly. He only
agreed that he taught the annihilation of Greed, Aversion and
Delusion.

As to 'the person who enters Nibbana,' we have seen already that
as 'person' is only conventional truth, one should really speak of 'a
continuity of void processes.' It is needless to say that despite this
bare and uncheering phrase to describe a person, the enlightened
sage is not in any way to be characterized as dried-up or as

functioning only by a sort of transcendental clockwork. Some Buddhists, unassured, have speculated about a Seed of Enlightenment buried under the layers of mud, which are the accumulated impressions of kamma, awaiting favorable times for fruition. But we should remember, the Buddha advises practice and condemns speculation. Therefore we should clearly understand why he has taught about No-self. He was not interested in making general statements of a metaphysical nature such as the bald pronouncement sometimes seen: "There is no self." This is merely a speculative view. Neither was he interested in formulating doctrines and dogmas such as "You must believe that there is no self." Such is the grasping for emotional support at a speculative view. Out of his Great Compassion, he certainly made great efforts to show people the way beyond all dukkha. The Teaching of No-self is of central importance to the Way, it is useful, it is very practical. This is why it has been taught. Abandoning all one's views, one arrives after Insight, at the realization in the heart that this is the truth. Ultimately speaking: No one enters Nibbana, because there is no one to do so, no 'thing' to enter, and entry therefore impossible. Words have failed again. An ancient verse says:

> *Nibbana is, but not the person that enters it; The path is but no traveller on it is seen.*
>
> Visuddhi-Magga, XVI

It should hardly be necessary now to stress that Nibbana is not a place, sphere or realm of existence. The naive or uneducated may think of it in this way but there is little support for this. It is thus not to be equated with 'going to heaven' as the heaven-states are very definitely places, not above us somewhere up in the sky but above in a spiritual sense (see, I, Levels and Perceptions). Nibbana, in fact, lies outside space-time: it is no place and therefore not to be pointed out by direction and it is timeless as the moment of its experience lies outside time. It is infinite in all respects being without beginning or end, for it is the nature of reality itself. Even among those great sages who have known it, for them it has no beginning since they say that it is like discovering something which has always been true.

Many sages of the Buddhist tradition have time and again pointed out to people who were looking for Nibbana 'outside' and perhaps in the future, that it was nowhere but here and now. The Buddha himself once instructed a disciple that the Truth was to be found, not by going to the ends of the world, but within this six-foot body. It is our wrong processes of thought which prevent us from seeing it in the present moment: our delusion of a person, 'myself', obstructs the view. We are told in many a poetic declaration of Final Knowledge, how much more wonderful the world is once that obstruction has gone. Many a disciple has exclaimed at the moment of Enlightenment, how simple and yet how profoundly marvellous is the change which has now come about. It is evidently rather like a person who has spent all their life so far viewing the world in a distorting mirror—and then looks at it directly for the first time; or it is sometimes compared to one who wakes up from a peculiar world of dreams, and then realizes the perverted nature of them with the clarity of waking consciousness. For the ordinary person therefore, the birth-and-death world and the ideal, Nibbana, must seem very far apart: the sage (as a Buddha or Arahant) sees things differently and for such a one they are not different, the first depending on the presence of the Unwholesome Roots, Inversions, etc., and the other upon unobstructed Insight.

The Sage Upasiva once asked the Buddha about the condition of one attained to Nibbana, (one who has reached the goal):

Does one not exist who's reached the goal? (=annihilationism)
Or does one dwell forever free from ill? (=eternalism)
O Sage, do well declare this unto me
For certainly this dhamma's known to you.

The Buddha replied:

Of one who's reached the goal no measure's found,
There is not that by which one could be named;
When dhammas for that one have been destroyed,
Destroyed are all the ways of telling too.

This brief presentation of some features of the Dhamma which has been taught by the Perfectly Enlightened One, may be brought to a close with an aspiration found in one of the classical biographies of the Great Teacher:

"May we, having crossed, lead others across; ourselves free, set others free; ourselves comforted, give comfort to others; ourselves released, give release to others. May this come to pass for the welfare and happiness of the multitude, out of compassion for the world, for the sake of the great multitude, and for the welfare and happiness of gods and men."

EVAM
May it be so indeed.

PĀLI AND SANSKRIT EQUIVALENTS OF WORDS MARKED WITH AN ASTERISK IN THE TEXT

The writer is aware that some will disagree with the idea of leaving most non-English words out of the text. In doing so, he has warned readers that they miss much of the richness of Buddhist thought, and trusts that those who wish to carry on with Buddhist studies will at least learn a few of these key words. A technical subject requires a technical vocabulary: Buddhism dealing with the Enlightenment of the mind is certainly a technical subject in this respect. Sanskrit forms of these terms, where different, follow the Pali in brackets. Occasionally the Thai words based upon either the Pali or the Sanskrit have been given.

Page

1.	Teachings	*Dhamma (Dharma)*
1.	faith, confidence	*saddhā (śraddhā)*
2.	come-and-see	*ehipassiko*
2.	leading inwards	*opanayiko*
2.	each intelligent person for themselves	*paccattaṁ veditabbo viññūhi.*
4.	noble-friend	*kalyāna-mitta (kalyānamitra)*
4.	Freedom	*vimutti (vimukti)*
5.	Enlightenment	*Bodhi*
6.	Best among humanity	*uttamapurisa*
7.	timeless	*akāliko*
7.	perfection	*pārami (paramita)*

Page

12.	unknowing, ignorance	*avijjā (avidyā)*
12.	the wandering-on	*saṁsāra*
13.	god	*deva, devata*
14.	Sage of the Sakyas	*Sakiyamuni (Śākyamuni)*
14.	destruction of the taints	*āsavakkhaya-ñāṇa* *(aśravakṣaya jñāna)*

15. All *sabbam (sarvaṁ)* meaning: eye, sight-object, and eye-consciousness, and similar triplets for the other senses, to mind, mental objects, and mind- consciousness. All that is knowable is here included.

15. *dhamma (dharma)*, all the experiencable events which may be classified with the above 18 elements or into more complex patterns.

16.	Turning the Wheel of Dhamma	*Dhammacakkappavattana Sutta (Dharmacakrapravartana Sūtra)*
16.	monk	*bhikkhu (bhikṣu)*
16.	Stream-entry	*Sotāpatti (śrota-āpatti)*
16.	Arahant (perfected one)	*arahant (arhat)*
16.	Order of Buddhist Monks	*bhikkhu-saṅgha*
16.	Order of Buddhist Nuns	*bhikkhunī-saṅgha (bhikṣunī)*
17.	ordinary person	*puthujjana (pṛithagjana)*

17. *"Handadāni bhikkhave āmantayāmi vo, vayadhammā saṅ khārā, appāmadena sampādethā' ti"*

17.	concentration	*jhāna (dhyāna)*
17.	Nibbana-which-leaves-nothing behind	*anupādisesa-nibbana (nirvana)*
17.	reliquary mounds, later monuments	*thūpa, cetiya (stupa, caitya,* Thai: *satup, chedi)*
19.	Books of Discipline	*Vinaya Piṭaka (Thai: Winai,* spells *Vinai)*
19.	Discourses of the Buddha and his disciples	*Sutta Piṭaka (sutra, Thai: Sut)*

Page

19.	Books of Psychological Analysis and Synthesis	*Abhidhamma Pitaka (Abhidharma*, Thai: *Abhidham)*
20.	wholesome means	*upaya-kosalla (kausalya)*
22.	unsatisfactoriness, suffering	*dukkha (duhkha, Thai: took)*
23.	craving	*tanhā (triśnā)*
26.	five groups:	*pañcakhandha (panca-skandha)*
	-form (physical and subtle)	*-rūpa*
	-feeling	*-vedanā*
	-memory/recognition	*-saññā (samjna)*
	-thoughts	*-sankhārā (samskārah)*
	-consciousness	*-vinnana (vijnana)*
29.	One who has discovered the just-so-ness of everything	*Tathagata*
30.	dukkha's arising	*dukkha-nirodha*
30.	its cessation	*dukkha-samudaya*
30.	the Way leading to its cessation	*Dukkha-nirodhagāminī patipadā (pratipadā)*
31.	action	*kamma (karma)*
31.	results	*vipāka, phala*
31.	wholesome and unwholesome action	*kusala and akusala kamma*
33.	dependent arising	*paticca-samuppāda (pratitya-samutpāda)*
35.	again-being	*punabbhava (punarbhava)*
39.	relinking consciousness	*patisandhi-viññāṇa*
39.	stream of existence	*santati*
49.	titan	*asura*
50.	human being	*manussa (manuṣya)*
52.	hungry ghosts	*peta (preta*, Thai: *pret)*
53.	animals	*tiracchāna (tiryagyoni)*

Page
54.	hells	*niraya (naraka, Thai: narok)*
58.	aeon	*kappa (kalpa)*
59.	galaxy	*cakkavāla (cakravala)*
61.	world	*loka*
65.	mental states (mind, heart)	*citta*
65.	mental factors	*cetasika (caitta-dharmaḥ)*
67.	roots of evil	*akusala mūla*
67.	inversions-inverted views	*vipallāsa (viparyāsa)*
71.	impermanence	*anicca (anitya)*
71.	no-self	*anattā (anātma)*
71.	three marks of existence *t*	*ilakkhana (trilakṣana)*
		Sabbe saṅkhārā aniccā
		Sabbe saṅkhārā dukkhā
		Sabbe dhammā anattā
71.	clear-seeing, insight	*vipassanā (vipaśyanā)*
73.	merit	*puñña (punya, Thai: boon)*
73.	-perfections	*-pārami (pāramitā)*
	-renunciation	*-nekkhamma (naiśkramya)*
	-aspiration	*-panidhāna (pranidhāna)*
	-giving	*-dāna*
	-virtue	*-sīla (śīla)*
	-patience	*-khanti (kṣānti)*
	-energy	*-viriya (vīrya)*
	-collectedness	*-samādhi*
	-wisdom	*-paññā (prajñā)*
	-wholesome means	*-upaya-kosalla (upayakauśalya)*
	-truth	*-sacca (satya)*
76.	Middle Path of Practice	*majjhimapatipada (madhyamapratipad)*
80.	monks' code	*pāṭimokkha (prātimokṣa)*
81.	Noble One, developed person	*Ariya (Ārya)*

Page

81.	defilements	*kilesa (kleśa)*
83.	hearing (and reading) wisdom	*suta-maya-paññā (prajñā)*
83.	thinking wisdom	*cinta-maya-paññā*
83.	developed wisdom	*bhāvana-maya-paññā*
90.	Virtue, morality	*sīla (śīla)*
90.	rules (or steps) of training	*sikkhāpada (sikṣāpada)*
90.	Five Precepts	*Pañca-sīla*
96.	shame	*hiri (hrī)*
96.	fear of evil	*ottappa (apatrapa)*
97.	world-guardians	*lokapāla*
97.	wisdom	*paññā (prajñā)*
97.	compassion	*karunā*
97.	five ennobling virtues:	*pañca kalyanadhamma*
	-loving-kindness	*-mettā (maitrī)*
	-right livelihood	*-sammā ājīva*
	-contentment	*-santutthi*
	-truthfulness	*-sacca (satya)*
	-mindfulness, awareness	*-appamāda (apramāda)*
98.	eight precepts	*attha sīla (Aṣṭasīla)*
99.	ten precepts	*dasa sīla*
99.	novice	*sāmaṇera (śramanera)*
101.	mental development	*bhāvana*
101.	one-pointedness	*ekaggatā (ekagratā)*
101.	concentration	*jhāna (dhyāna)*
102.	five hindrances	*pañca nīvaraṇa*
103.	mindfulness	*sati (smṛti)*
104.	happiness and joy	*sukha and pīti (prīti)*
104.	equanimity	*upekkhā (upekṣā)*
104.	Magical Abilitics	*iddhi (ṛiddhi)*
107.	greed	*lobha*
107.	aversion	*dosa (dveśa)*
107.	delusion	*moha*

Page

106. intelligence   *buddhi*

106. discursiveness   *vitakka (vitarka)*

108. The 32 parts of the body are: *Kesā*–hair of the head, *lomā*–
      hair of the body, *nakhā*–nails, *dantā*–teeth, *taco*–skin,
      mamsam–flesh, *nahāru*–sinews, *aṭṭhi*–bones, *aṭṭhimiñjam*–
      bone-marrow, *vakkam*–kidneys, *hadayam*–heart, *yakanam*–
      liver, *kilomakam*–membranes, *pihakam*–spleen, *papphāsam*–
      lungs, *antam*–large gut, *antagunam*–small gut, *udariyam*–
      gorge, *karīsam*–dung, *pittam*–bile, *semham*–phlegm, *pubbo*–
      pus, *lohitam*–blood, *sedo*–sweat, *medo*–fat, *assu*–tears, *vasā*–
      skin-grease, *khelo*–spittle, *singhānikā*–snot, *lasikā*–oil of the
      joints, *muttam*–urine, (*mattha-lungam*–brain in the skull.
      This last one is not in many lists which give only 31 parts).
      Note that these parts are not to be taken as an anatomically
      complete description of this body but have been specially
      selected by the Buddha as being suitable objects to stimulate
      revulsion regarding the body, thus enabling the essential
      detachment from concepts of 'me-mine' respecting the body
      to take place. Revulsion (equanimity) towards the body (a
      wholesome mental state) must not be confused with hatred
      against the body, (a very unwholesome state of mind).

110. *"asmim sati, idam hoti: imass' uppādā, idam uppajjati:*
      imasmim asati, idam na hoti: imassa nirodhā, idam nirujjhati."

111. mindfulness of breathing   *ānāpāna-sati (ānāprāna-smṛti)*

120. divine abidings   *brahma-vihāra*

121. loving-kindness   *mettā*

121. compassion   *karunā*

121. gladness   *muditā*

121. equanimity   *upekkhā*

128. contentment   *santutthi*

129. gratitude, requititude   *kataññu-katavedi*

129. humility   *nivāta*

133. one who knows,   *jānatā, passatā*
      one who sees

Page
134.	supermundane wisdom	*lokuttara-paññā*
135.	relative truth	*sammutti-sacca (saṁvṛtti-satya)*
135.	Ultimate Truth	*paramattha-sacca (paramartha-satya)*
145.	foolish worlding	*bala-puthujjana*
145.	beautiful worlding	*kalyāna-pathujjana*
145.	stream-enterer	*sotāpanna*

LIST OF BOOKS FOR FURTHER READING

Books marked with an asterisk are printed in Thailand.

ON BUDDHISM GENERALLY

The Life of the Buddha, Ven. Nyanamoli Thera, B.P.S., Kandy.

Old Path, White Clouds, Thich Nhat Hanh, Parallax Press, Berkeley, CA 1985.

*What the Buddha Taught, Ven. W. Rahula. Hawtrai Foundation, Bangkok.

Liberation in the Palm of Your Hand, Pabongka Rinpoche, Wisdom Publications, Somerville, MA, U.S.A., 1997.

*The Dhammapada, Jewels within the Heart, Silkworm Books, Chiang Mai, 1999.

A Concise History of Buddhism, Andrew Skilton, Windhorse Publications, Birmingham, U.K.

The Three Jewels: An Introduction to Buddhism, Sangharakshita, Windhorse Publications, Birmingham, U.K.

The Word of the Buddha, by Ven. Nyanatiloka Thera, B.P.S.

A Guide to Buddhist Path, Sangharakshita, Windhorse Publications, Birmingham, U.K.

The Heart of Buddhist Meditation, by Ven. Nyanaponika Thera, Rider and Co. London.

Buddhism, Its Essence and Development, by Dr. E Conze, Bruno Cassirer, Oxford.

Buddhist Texts through the Ages (anthology), ed. Conze, Bruno Cassirer.

Buddhist Scriptures (anthology), trans. Conze, Penguin Books.

A Dictionary of Buddhist Terms, by Ven. Nyanatiloka, B.P.S.

The Mirror: Advice on the Presence of Awareness, Namkhai, Station Hill Openings, Barrytown, N.Y., U.S.A., 1996.

BOOKS BY THE SAME AUTHOR

Tolerance, A Study from Buddhist Sources

Calm and Insight, a Buddhist Manual for Meditators, Curzon Press, London.

Banner of the Arahants, Buddhist monks and nuns from the Buddha's time till now, B.P.S.

Pointing to Dhamma, 30 Buddhist Discourses given at Wat Bovoranives over a period of three years, Mahamakut Press.

Buddha my Refuge an anthology from the Buddha's discourses on his Nine Virtues.

A Criterion of True Religion, Lord Buddha's Discourse to the Kalama people, translated from Pali with a Commentary, Mahamakut Press.

The Dharma-flavour, a book of poems: published privately.

With Robes and Bowl, The forest bhikkhu's life, B.P.S.

A Visakha Offering. Eight wonderful qualities of the Exalted Buddha, B.P.S.

Practical Advice for Meditators, (the chapters on meditation from this book.), B.P.S.

The Buddhist Monk's Discipline. Some points explained for lay people, B.P.S.

The Wheel of Birth and Death, full explanation of the diagram in this book, B.P.S.

Brief Advice to those who wish to Go Forth to Homelessness as Buddhist Monks, (see last chapter of "Banner of the Arahants.")

COMPILER OF:

Patimokkha, the 227 Fundamental Rules of a Buddhist Monk.

The Splendour of Enlightenment, a Life of the Buddha, in 2 volumes compiled from many sources, Mahamakut Press.

A Treasury of the Buddha's Words, ninety Discourses from the Middle
Collection in 3 volumes, translated by Ven. Nyanamoli,
Mahamakut Press.

His Majesty King Rama the Fourth Mongkut. Centenary Volume,
Mahamakut Press.

The Buddha's Last Bequest, an account from the Chinese of His last
discourse, B.P.S.

TRANSLATOR OF:

Jewels Within the Heart, a translation of the Dhammapada with
introductory essays. Silkworm Books, Chiang Mai (forthcoming).

CO-TRANSLATOR OF:

The Opening of the Wisdom-Eye, by H. H. the Dalai Lama,
Theosophical Publishing house, U.S.A.

The Entrance to the Vinaya, Vol. I, II, III. A recent Commentary
on the Buddhist monks' Discipline, Mahamakut Press.

ADDRESSES FOR BUDDHIST BOOKS

PALI TEXT SOCIETY (P.T.S.)
73 Lime Walk, Headington,
Oxford, OX3 7AD, England.

BUDDHIST PUBLICATION SOCIETY (B.P.S.)
P.O. Box 61, Kandy, Sri Lanka.

ASPECTS OF BUDDHISM IN THAILAND

The writer has been asked to add to the second edition an account of Buddhism in Thailand to supplement the general survey of Buddhist Teachings given in the rest of the book. This is particularly difficult to do in a short space and really requires a book in itself. However, in this outline three points have been taken, around which some idea of Thai Buddhist organization and practice may be gained. These three are: types of Buddhist, festivals celebrated by Buddhists and some brief observations upon the architectural features of the wats (*avasa*, Buddhist "monasteries")[1] and their practical functions.

First then come Buddhists as people. As shown in the section on the Sangha (What do Buddhists Practise?), there are four groups of Buddhists comprising the Buddhist Community: *bhikkhus* (monks), *bhikkhunis* (nuns) *upasakas* (laymen) and *upasikas* (laywomen). It has been related already how the bhikkhunis in Theravada[2]

---

1. In this account the Thai names are given first followed by the Pali in brackets and an English translation.

2. Theravada: The Way of the Elders, the teachings and practice based upon the Pali texts and their commentaries. They are admitted to contain some of the oldest accounts of the Dhamma (teachings) and Vinaya (discipline) now found. Theravada traditions are strong in Thailand, Burma, Sri Lanka, Laos, Cambodia, with considerable following in Malaysia, Vietnam and Bangladesh, and growing interest in India, Indonesia and Europe.

countries, have ceased to exist, so that in Thailand we find only the three other groups with pious laywomen living as 8-precept nuns or *mae chi*.

Among bhikkhus (monks) often known as "Phra" (*vara*, excellent) there are various divisions based upon traditions of ordination and practice. Theravada bhikkhus fall into four groups. The largest of these, Mahanikai (*Mahanikaya*, the Great Division) to which the great majority of wats in Thailand are joined, represents the old Thai ordination tradition stemming originally from Sri Lanka. Due to the terrible havoc caused by the Burmese invasion and the sacking of Ayutthaya (C.E. 1767), many undesirable persons were ordained or posed as bhikkhus. This led to a great decline in learning and practice of Dhamma and Vinaya, and such a low level was reached that civil officers were specially empowered to beat bhikkhus who were found infringing the training-rules of the Vinaya. This state of affairs continued into the third reign of the present dynasty, in spite of the great efforts made by the kings through their edicts to reform and properly regulate the Sangha (order). During the third reign, Prince Mongkut who had been temporarily ordained according to Thai practice for one Rainy-Season, found that he could not gain success in the meditation exercises to which he at first devoted himself and began to suspect that practice as well as conduct and scholarship were far sundered from the ideals of Gotama the Buddha. At first contemplating returning to lay-life, disheartened by the uninspiring state of the Sangha, at this crucial time he met a senior bhikkhu from the Mon tradition who impressed him very greatly as he practised the Vinaya strictly and was well-learned in Dhamma. Prince Mongkut then took re-ordination into the Mon tradition and having become proficient in Pali language (or Magadhi, the language in which the Discourses and Discipline have been preserved), he was appointed by order of his half-brother King Rama III, the abbot of a new temple (Wat Bovoranives). From his grasp of the principles taught in the original texts and by his strict practice of those principles, together with popular expositions of

Dhamma in Thai which ordinary people could understand, he collected about him a body of bhikkhus who admired his sincerity, honesty and close adherence to the original teachings of the Buddha. This group having a different ordination lineage later came to be known as Thammayutnikai (*Dhammayuttika-nikaya*, those who adhere to Dhamma).

Subsequently, Mahanikai made efforts to purify itself and to cast out unworthy practices. It still remains true to say however, that most Thammayut temples insist upon care and attention to even small points in the bhikkhus' training while such is not always the case in Mahanikai. In present-day Thailand, Mahanikai bhikkhus are found in the ratio of 37 to 1 to Thammayut bhikkhus. Usually it is not possible to distinguish bhikkhus of these groups by their dress, although in temples adhering to the original Thai traditions (old Mahanikai) there is a special way of wearing the upper robe.

Between bhikkhus, of these two main groups (see below), there is harmony and much invitation by each group of the other upon all occasions except those involving some formal act of the Sangha (*sanghakamma*, as in ordination). Most laypeople have no attachment to a particular group, so that it is wrong to speak of "sects". The differences that exist in strictness of practice are matters for bhikkhus alone.

Brief mention should also be made of Mon and Burmese temples. Most Mon temples are administered through Thammayut but they have distinct traditions such as using Mon pronunciation of Pali. Burmese temples are found mostly in Chiang Mai and Lampang in northern Thailand.

Another category helpful for understanding Thai Buddhist practice is "pariyat" and "patibat". The first means "thorough learning" and characterizes the practice of town-bhikkhus. They learn, often as novices, the Dhamma first in Thai and then having passed through three examinations, begin the learning of Pali in which there are nine grades. Their daily routine begins with perhaps meditation individually, then walking to collect alms when it is light, eating the first meal, chanting in the temple, lessons in the Pali school of the wat, eating the last meal (at about eleven in the morning), a rest followed by more lessons and then, sometime in the late afternoon or evening, another chanting in the main temple. The remainder of the day is there for individual study. However, many things may happen to interrupt this pattern. Laypeople may invite bhikkhus for either of the meals and often for chanting in houses, while in the afternoons visitors and members of the family from which the bhikkhu comes may call upon him. Ceremonies and festivals may also intervene, (see page 152).

The "patibat" or practice bhikkhu is usually a forest-dweller, especially in the case of Thammayut practice bhikkhus. Such as the latter live in forest temples often far from villages and lead highly disciplined lives since there can be no attainment of collectedness *(samadhi)* until moral practice is very pure. In a forest temple days go by without interruption and with few variations. Typical would be the following: **meditation**, both sitting and walking in the early hours of the morning, meeting in the "hall" *(sala)* before setting out to collect alms, eating the almsfood with the hand from the bowl (there is only one meal), return to the individual huts for work or practice, sweeping the whole wat in the afternoon, cleaning the sala, carrying water to the water jars outside huts and in lavatories, bathing round the well, a sweet drink (sometimes) and in the evening, except when the Teacher calls a meeting for instruction of bhikkhus, the remainder of the night is given to individual meditation practice until sleep become absolutely necessary.* Mahanikai meditation centres are more often found near towns or in them and the training principles adopted seem in most places less arduous. Many patibat bhikkhus do not know Pali well, having never studied it formally but instead of opening the books of the

---

* For bhikkhu forest life in detail, see my *With Robes and Bowl* (Buddhist Publication Society, Kandy, Sri Lanka. For both kinds of Bhikkhu-life in much more detail see *Banner of the Arathants,* also from B.P.S.

scriptures, they are encouraged by their Teachers who have already travelled along the Path they teach, to make efforts to open the book of Dhamma which lies within, since the nature of materiality (body) and mentality is the nature of Dhamma.

Nuns are also found learned in Dhamma, some passing through the Dhamma examinations while others devote their time to meditation in quiet and secluded places. Many nuns however do not live in any community and may be widows, old women seeking shelter of a religious life and having little education. Numbers of them spend much time making *punya* (merit, see page 152) by preparing food for bhikkhus, clearing the wat area and so on.

Coming now to laymen and laywomen, their five precepts have been mentioned already (and see Appendix II). What else do they practise? Those who are devoted go to the *wats* on Uposatha days and holy days *(wan phra)* perhaps presenting food to bhikkhus, then undertaking the Eight Precepts in the main temple, listening to the Dhamma-exposition, perhaps meditation through the day, or reading Dhamma-books and generally spending the day quietly within the precincts of the wat. Apart from their participation in various festivals (see page 153), laypeople are often encouraged to practise ten aspects of "making *punya*" *(tham bun)*.[3] These have already been mentioned briefly and form the subject of a booklet by the writer in which he has dealt with the how and why of making punya.[4] Lay Buddhists in all Buddhist lands are particularly keen upon this aspect of Dhamma which can really transform people so that they become deeply religious and wonderfully happy. The words *tham bun* are heard everywhere in Thailand and it is the practice which enables "Every evil never doing" to go along with "And in wholesomeness increasing." One should remark here that meditation is also counted as one way of increasing wholesomeness

3. Punya means "those actions which clean and purify the mind" of the one doing them. A very inadequate translation is "merit".

4. See 'The Advantages of Merit', *Bodhi Leaves* B.38, B.P.S.

and therefore as a way of making *punya*. The most devoted laypeople have a meditation Teacher and practise everyday early in the morning and perhaps before sleeping. Far from being merely insignificant, lay participation in Dhamma-practice is so varied as to defy inclusion in this brief notice and it is only scholars who have never been to Buddhist countries who can talk about the Dhamma as though it was for bhikkhus only!

Before passing on to festivals, it should be noted that there are two groups of Mahayana Buddhists[5] in Thailand. The most numerous are the Chinese who have many temples, some having resident bhikkhus and some being the centres of lay Buddhist societies. Chinese bhikkhus are easily distinguished from those of Theravada as in Thailand they wear an orange jacket and trousers with a robe over one shoulder. They are vegetarians and never go out to collect alms, their food being prepared in the temple. They conduct an elaborate, by Theravada standards, *puja* (ceremonial reverence) twice a day in their temples early in the morning (4 a.m.) and again in the afternoon at four. Their temples which are typically Chinese in style usually have three Buddhas seated side by side-representing the Buddhas of past (Dipamkara), Present (Gotama) and future (Ariyametteyya) together with the attendant bhikkhus Mahakassapa and Ananda, and some of the bodhisattvas. Their services are much sought by the Chinese community for death-ceremonies. Among them one may find some who understand Dhamma well. The other group are called "Yuan" that is, Vietnamese people who, a long time ago, fled to Thailand and settled here. Their group of monks are a sort of half-way house between the Chinese and Theravada. While wearing robes like the Chinese, they do go out for alms-collecting and are not strict

5. Mahayana, (lit: the Great Vehicle), an ancient development brought about and certainly maintained by historical accidents. While Mahayana scriptures often look very different compared to those of Theravada in practice the two branches is really very similar.

vegetarians (except some who wish to be, as in Theravada). They have teachers among them with detailed knowledge of *mantras* (words of power) and *mudras* (hand-gestures) which are used in a kind of tantric ceremonial especially upon the Chinese Half-year when there is the Great Giving (Mahatan-*mahadana*) when besides mortal men, the hungry ghosts are also invited and fed (called "Bon" Festival in Japan from the Sanskrit '*avalambana*', pitying).

The second aspect of Thai Buddhist practice is the festivals. Those mentioned here are all celebrated throughout the country but there are others having only a local range. Beginning with the "old" Thai New Year, these festivals follow through the months:

1. Songkran, Thai New Year on the thirteenth of April. There is great almsgiving to bhikkhus in the early morning. Then the bone-relics of ancestors may be taken to the wat where there will be chanting by bhikkhus and punya made by laypeople in the name of those dead persons, to aid them in their new birth. Robes presented at this time are called *bang-sakun (pamsakula civara)* for although very rarely made from cloth wrapping the dead body, they are accepted by the bhikkhus invited to take them, chanting a reflection upon death. This ceremony is also performed in the houses of laypeople who invite bhikkhus for this occasion. Another feature of the New Year is the carrying of sand into the grounds of the wat and making with it *phra chedi* (*cetiya, stupa*, reliquary monuments) placing around them all sorts of gifts which bhikkhus are invited to take. The idea of bringing sand is that on leaving the grounds of the wat one takes away soil adhering to one's shoes. Since it is thought wrong to remove anything from a wat, once a year the soil is replaced in the form of clean sand which can be swept easily. In some places also there is the pouring of water over special Buddha-images and even on bhikkhus with the idea of showing respect.

2. Visakha puja (*Wesak* in Sri Lanka) Buddha Day, the anniversary of the birth, enlightenment and final quenching of the

Buddha in the sixth month of Visakha upon the full-moon day. Like all other festivals, it begins with extensive almsgiving to bhikkhus in the early morning while in the afternoon school children circumambulate the phra chedi under the guidance of bhikkhus and teachers. In the evening after long chanting bhikkhus headed by the abbot and elders, take flowers, lighted incense and candles and solemnly circumambulate the phra cedi in which are kept relics of the Great Teacher. When thrice circled (once recollecting the Buddha, once Dhamma, once Sangha) it is the turn of laypeople who come to large temples in the thousands. They perform also this triple circumambulation and then (some of them) join bhikkhus to hear all-night chanting alternating with expositions of Dhamma. Some practise meditation as well. The Buddhist Era dates from the Parinibbana (Final Quenching) of the Buddha and has now (1998) reached the year 2541 (=2542, Sri Lanka).

3. Thawai phra phloeng (lit: Giving the Fire), seven days after Visakha Puja in commemoration of the cremation of Lord Buddha's body at the time when Venerable Mahakassapa had arrived at the pyre. It is said that the fire could not be lighted until this time. Fewer laypeople come to the temple for the triple circumambulation which is performed by all bhikkhus as described above. Some temples have Dhamma-expositions and chanting all night.

4. Buat Nak, giving *Upasampada* (higher ordination) to *Naga* (aspirant to ordination). In the village these ceremonies begin in April-May with the "rains-bhikkhus" remaining in robes until the beginning of the rains-residence (Phansa—see page 174), while in the towns, June is the ordination season with rains-bhikkhus spending the rains-residence and returning to lay life in October or November. This custom applies mostly to pariyat and village wats since few men are ordained temporarily in patibat wats. In effect, this custom is a concentrated course for learning about Dhamma and Vinaya, that is the teachings and the discipline which supports them. Most of those ordained are young, just over the age of 20 (since conception) but a number of older men take this opportunity to learn Dhamma and to make punya out of gratitude to their parents, a chance which they may not have had when young. Government servants as well as those permitted to do so in the armed forces are given leave with full pay for four months, once in their lives, so that they may train in the way of Dhamma. The ceremony falls into two parts: the lay rituals and festivities held in the home of the *nak* including sometimes a colourful and musical procession to the temple, and the solemn ordination proceedings within. In some cases the *nak* is dressed as a prince and follows the pattern of Gotama's going-forth. The ceremony within the temple also consists of two parts: the Going-forth *(pabbajja)* of the white-clad *nak* to become a *nen* (*samanera*, or novice) and the acceptance (*upasampada*) of that nain to become a *bhikkhu*. The bhikkhus are all seated surrounding the abbot upon a platform while the laypeople—parents, relatives and friends, sit upon the floor. At the conclusion of the ceremony, presents are given to the abbot and teachers of the new bhikkhu and gifts distributed to the other witnessing bhikkhus.

5. **Asalhapuja**, Dhamma Day, the anniversary of the first teaching of Dhamma in the Deer Sanctuary at Benares, 2,586 years ago (in 1998). This takes place on the Full Moon of the eighth month one day before Khao Phansa (see below). There is almsgiving in the morning and chanting by bhikkhus in the evening of the Buddha's first Discourse called Revolving the Wheel of Dhamma. Afterwards, flowers, candles and incense are offered at the phra cedi and following this there is an exposition of Dhamma for bhikkhus and laypeople in the temple.

6. **Wan Khao Phansa** (Rains-entry Day, the Rains-residence). In the afternoon, laypeople come to the temple and forming a long

line, present flowers, incense and candles to all bhikkhus and samaneras who will enter upon the rains-residence in the wat. All Buddha-images, phra cedi and relics are then revered by bhikkhus who make a tour of the sacred area of the wat for this purpose. In the evening all bhikkhus meet in the temple and after being exhorted by the abbot, recite the formula binding themselves to observe the discipline of phansa. They beg forgiveness of each other before returning to their dwellings. During the three months of Pansa there is an intensification of Buddhist activity, **more** meditation, **more** study, **more** almsgiving, **more** listening to Dhamma, etc.

7. **Wan Sat** (*Sraddha*–offerings of the departed) falling in the tenth month (October) and commemorating the Half-year in the old calendar. One is grateful to be alive still and in gratitude remembers one's ancestors. Assuming that some of them have been born as hungry ghosts, food offerings placed upon special banana-leaf trays are taken to the crossroads. They are left there by members of the family after dedicating them for the use of the ghosts in question. One must not look back as one returns to the house! In the south of Thailand this becomes two festivals separated by a week, in the first of which ghosts are invited back to their former homes where punya is made in their names, sometimes for all the seven days, after which they are respectfully requested to return to their abodes.

8. **Wan Ok Phansa** (Rains-end Day), a monastic ceremony in which laypeople do not participate. Bhikkhus are free after *pavarana* to travel and stay at other temples.

9. **Wan Pavarana** (Admonition Day). This day follows Ok Phansa and all the bhikkhus who have spent the rains-residence together invite other bhikkhus to admonish them if they have seen, heard or suspected any wrong-doing upon their part. There is a feeling of great gladness and friendliness among all.

10. Tot Kathin (*Kathina*, taking special robes). In the month following Ok Phansa there is great activity among laypeople up and down the country. During phansa one layperson has arranged with the abbot of a wat to take charge of the presentation of kathina robes (except in some royal wats where H.M. the King or his representative always presents kathin). These robes, together with a great variety of other requisites which have been collected by the laypeople are taken in procession on foot, by lorry and bus over long distances or most enjoyably by water to the wat and there made over to the Sangha. This form of making *punya* is esteemed above others since the chance to perform it only occurs once in a year. The new robes (one set of three robes) are then formally made over to a bhikkhu agreed upon by the Sangha. This festival is very popular as it provides a good opportunity for making *punya* combined with sightseeing in distant parts of the country. 'Money-trees' for the wat's support are a prominent feature in this festival.

11. Tot Pha Pa (Taking forest cloth). At any time of the year but especially in the winter months, this is also popular. There are numbers of ways in which forest-cloth can be given. Most informal and anonymous is the placing of robes in a tree at night and then retreating letting off fire-crackers with much laughter to tell the bhikkhus that forest-cloth is there for the taking. Or a branch of tree may be brought in procession to the sala (see below) and there filled to overflowing with robes and other requisites. This method of offering otherwise resembles Tot Kathin.

12. Pi Mai (New Year's Day, January). Since the adoption of this day for beginning the year, Thais have had two New Year's Days to celebrate. There is bountiful alms giving and invitations for bhikkhus to chant in the houses of laypeople.

13. Wat Fairs. These are held usually during the winter on summer in order to raise funds for the building of temples, dwellings and other necessary structures. Some wats do not permit these annual events, which besides attracting crowds of people, also make a lot of noise. Patibat wats, for instance, where meditation is most important, never have such fairs.

14. **Magha Puja**, Sangha Day, the anniversary of the first recitation of the *Patimokkha* (the 227 fundamental rules of a bhikkhu) and celebrated in much the same way as Visakha Puja. It falls in the third or fourth lunar month (February or March).

15. **Trut**, approximately two weeks before the Songkran festival, is a sort of New Year's Eve, upon which occasion there is more *punya*-making.

Besides most of the above fixed festivals there are numerous other events for the making of punya by laypeople. For instance, birthdays (which Buddhists celebrate by giving gifts, not by expecting presents) and death anniversaries. The writer has been invited on several occasions to houses where ancestors dead forty or fifty years ago are still being honoured, remembered and *punya* made in their names. Similarly, with the very aged who are helped to give gifts upon their birthdays, or with the very young who are also helped by their mothers to give (at one year old inviting two bhikkhus to whom the baby 'gives'; at two, three bhikkhus, and so on). And sometimes when a person lies dying, bhikkhus are invited to chant so that he may hear the sound and gifts for them pass through his dying hands. All this is done so that people die in peace remembering the deeds of punya done by them and thus attain a good rebirth, while the young even in infancy are led to understand the great value of giving. Funerals are another occasion for this and a time when another sort of giving is practised. Guests invited to some cremations are given a book or books often upon some aspect of Dhamma, sometimes written by the deceased and sometimes reprints of Dhamma books till then out of print. Dhamma is also taught upon this occasion taking some text in which impermanence and death are the subjects. Except for those festivals of a monastic nature and the three great days honouring each of the Triple Gem, forest bhikkhus will not be concerned with many of the festivals mentioned here.

The third point to be discussed here is a brief summary of Thai Buddhist architecture. First, because oldest is the *phra chedi (cetiya, stupa)*, a monument containing either bodily relics of the Buddha, or else enshrining things used by him such as his bowl and so forth, or in the absence of either of these, enshrining palm leaf books inscribed with the Discourses he taught. The more important of these phra chedi are gilded, covered with Chinese tiles or kept spotlessly white-washed. They are honoured as symbols of the Buddha and like Buddha-images (and bhikkhus, kings and princes) are spoken of using the honorific classifier "ong". This honouring of phra cedi goes back to soon after the Parinibbana of the Buddha when his relics were divided and placed in eight mounds surmounted by the parasol of royalty. Great devotion is accorded to these Buddha-symbols, for while they remain in the world the Middle Practice-path remains but when they are no more seen then the path is closed and the world must wait for the coming of the future Buddha, Ariyametteyya.

Buddha-images have already been mentioned, the principal one in any wat being placed upon a high lotus throne in the main temple (*buat*—where ordination and other ceremonies are held). Frequently made of gilded bronze and occasionally solid gold, these symbols of the Buddha (they are not intended to show what he really looked like) are still being made in large numbers. This tradition of representing the Buddha as an image goes back some two thousand years. For some hundreds of years after his Parinibbana he was not represented except by symbols (a lotus bud for birth, a Bodhi-tree for the Enlightenment, his footprints for the Buddha's travels, a wheel for his teaching Dhamma and a phra cedi for his Parinibbana). Then Greek influence entered India in the wake of Alexander's conquests and Buddha-images began to be made. Why was he not represented at first? Readers may turn to the Buddha's reply to Upasiva, "Of one who's reached the goal no measure's found…"

In Thailand, the most revered of all Buddha-images is the Emerald Buddha enshrined in its great temple within the walls of the Grand Palace in Bangkok. It is carved from one piece of green jade and is many hundreds of years old.

The presiding Buddha-image is enshrined in the *bot*, a temple specially consecrated for the formal acts of the Sangha (such as ordination, reciting the Patimokkha, requesting admonition, etc.) It may be identified by eight stone markers placed at intervals around the outside of the building usually free-standing but sometimes fixed to the walls. Of all the buildings in the sacred enclosure, this one is the most used and the one containing the most treasures placed upon the shrine in front of the Buddha-image. Frequently, the latter has as its attendants, images of the supreme pair among the Buddha's disciples: Venerables Sariputta and Moggallana.

Some wats have one or more *wihan (vihara)*, more properly called the Buddha-Vihara, that is, the dwelling of the Buddha. Some specially large or revered Buddha-image is kept there. But a majority of wats combine this with the Buat and have another and different type of structure called the *sala*.

Both *bot* and *wihan* are brick (rarely stone) structures built on an ornamental foundation but the *sala* is usually wooden-framed, standing off the ground and supported by strong posts. It is used mostly for large gatherings of laypeople especially upon holy days when they will come bringing food for bhikkhus, receive the Eight Precepts, and listen to Dhamma expositions.

Traditional Thai bhikkhu-dwellings, called kuti, are also raised upon wooden "legs" and made entirely of wood, usually teak. They manage to last for two or three hundred years if well cared for, a very long time in the Thai climate. Each bhikkhu in his room has a small Buddha-image and shrine which is the focus for his devotions before sleeping and when awakening. Frequently a smaller room or his verandas are the dwelling of a boy or boys committed to his care by parents who wish that they should be educated in the wat school and learn good conduct from the bhikkhu who is their teacher.

Having covered the three points: Buddhists, their festivals and wat buildings we should conclude this brief survey of some aspects of Buddhism now to be seen in Thailand. It may be good to round this off with some of the Buddha's words on merit:

> *If one should some evil do*
> *then do it not again, again.*
> *Do not wish for it anew*
> *for evil grows to pain.*

> *If one should some merit make*
> *do it then again, again.*
> *One should wish for it anew*
> *for merit grows to joy.*

> *Think lightly not of evil:*
> *'It will not come to me',*
> *for by the falling of waterdrops*
> *a waterjar is filled:*
> *fools with evil fill themselves,*
> *gathering little by little.*

> *Think lightly not of merit:*
> *'It will not come to me',*
> *for by the falling of waterdrops*
> *a waterjar is filled.*
> *the wise with merit fill themselves,*
> *gathering little by little.*

One who's long away from home
returns in safety from afar,
friends, well-wishers, kinsmen too
are overjoyed at his return.

In the same way the merit done
when from this world to another gone
those merits then receive one there
as relatives a dear one come.

Dhammapada 117, 118, 121, 122, 219, 220

THREE REFUGES AND FIVE PRECEPTS

Many visitors to Thailand, as to other Buddhist countries, may very easily see lay Buddhists requesting and then being given the Three Refuges and Five Precepts by a monk. Seeing this, they might want to know what it was all about as they are formulated in Pali, the ancient religious language of the Southern Buddhist countries. For their help, the Refuges and Precepts are given here in the Pali language with translation and some other relevant information.

First, the Refuges and Precepts must be requested by those who wish thereby to declare themselves followers of the Exalted One, undertaking further to train themselves in the five specified ways of moral observance. The Refuges and Precepts may not be given without such a request being made; this is to ensure that all those who take the Precepts—not always all of the persons present in a gathering—that those who do so, really wish quite freely to take those rules of training upon themselves. This is an adequate safeguard against forced conversion of unwilling persons by over-zealous propagators, such a thing being very un-Buddhist. Then again, the request is made three times, this number being common in all manner of Buddhist ceremonies and pronouncements, thus making sure that every one is quite clear about what is being done and fully understands its purpose. Before doing this, all persons honour the Three Jewels by making a triple prostration and throughout the entire proceeding the hands are held together in the reverential gesture like a lotus bud; at heart level.

1. *Aham (mayam) bhante,*   *tisaranena*
   I(we) Venerable Sir,   with the Three Refuges-
   saha pañcasīlāni   *yācāmi (yācāma)*
   together with the Five precepts   I ask for (we ask for)
2. *Dutiyampi, aham...*
   for the second time, I...
3. *Tatiyampi, aham...*
   For the third time, I...

Or in English: Venerable Sir, I request the Three Refuges together with the Five Precepts. For the second time... For the third time...

The monk then says:
"Yam aham vadāmi, tam vadehi"
Whatever I say, you should repeat.
And the lay-person(s) responds:
"Āma, bhante." ·
Yes, Venerable Sir.
The monk then intones:
"Namo tassa Bhagavato Arahato Sammasāmbuddhassa." (3 times).

The laypeople repeat this very ancient formula of worship three times. The first time venerating the countless Buddhas of the past, the second time paying homage to the Buddha of the present (Gotama the Perfectly awakened), and third is for the reverence of those who will be Buddhas in the future (such as Ariya Metteyya Bodhisatta now awaiting in Tusita Heaven a suitable time to take birth here among men). In English, this reverential address to the Buddhas may be translated:
"Homage to the Exalted One, Arahant, Perfectly Enlightened by Himself"
In this way, the Great Compassion of the buddhas is remembered by the word "*Bhagavato*", their Great Purity when reciting "*Araha-to*", and that they have attained that sublime pinnacle of

Enlightenment, the Great Wisdom with the word, *"Sammā-sambuddhassa".*

Now follow the Refuges in the Buddha, the Dhamma and the Sangha. Each one is first intoned by a monk and then repeated by the laity:

> *"Buddhaṁ   saranaṁ   gacchāmi,*
> *Dhammaṁ   saranaṁ   gacchāmi,*
> *Sanghaṁ   saranaṁ   gacchāmi,*
> To the Buddha for Refuge (I) go
> To the Dhamma for Refuge (I) go
> To the Sangha for Refuge (I) go
> *Dutiyampi Buddhaṁ... Dhammaṁ... Sanghaṁ,*
> For the second time to the Buddha, Dhamma, Sangha.
> *Tatiyampi Buddhaṁ... Dhammaṁ... Sanghaṁ*
> For the third time..."

Pali word-order being some what different from English, the Refuges in the latter language are best phrased: "To the Buddha I go for Refuge", etc.

They are repeated three times in Pali, to make certain that those repeating them are fully mindful of what they are doing. In addition, while repeating them, upon the first repetition one thinks of Going for Refuge with one's mind. Upon the second, with one's speech, and while repeating them the third time, one goes for Refuge with one's body. These three, mind, speech and body, being the doors of action of a human being, including as they do all his action, all must go for Refuge to the Triple Gem. This is 'whole-heartedly' Going for Refuge but to do so merely by pressing together one's palms (body) or just by unmindfully droning out words (speech), these are really no refuges at all; because of this, the monk who is giving them, then says to the lay people thus: *"Tisaraṇagamanaṁ sampunnaṁ"*—The going to the Three Refuges is complete. And they reply: *"Āma, bhante"*;—Yes, Venerable Sir.

Being assured that they are properly established in the Three Refuges, for the Precepts should not be given to those who have not faith in the Buddha, Dhamma and Sangha, the monk proceeds to chant the Five Precepts, each one of which the laypeople repeat after him.

1. *Pāṇatipātā veramaṇī sikkhāpadaṃ samādiyāmi* (beings-destruction of, refraining from, training, steps of, I undertake) or in English order which completely reverses the Pali: I undertake the rule of training to refrain from destroying beings

2. *Adinnādānā veramaṇī sikkhāpadaṃ samādiyāmi* (not taking not- given) I undertake the rule of training to refrain from taking what is not given.

3. *Kāmesu micchācārā veramaṇī sikkhāpadaṃ samādiyāmi* (in sexual-desires wrong conduct) I undertake the rule of training to refrain from wrong-doing in sexual desires.

4. *Musāvādā veramaṇī sikkhāpadaṃ samādiyāmi* (false speech) I undertake the rule of training to refrain from false speech.

5. *Sura-meraya-majja-pamādaṭṭhānā veramaṇī sikkhāpadaṃ samā diyāmi* (distilled, fermented, intoxicants, heedlessness-producing) I undertake the rule of training to refrain from distilled and fermented intoxicants which produce heedlessness.

Upon the laity repeating this last Precept, the monk then chants a passage showing the benefits of keeping these Precepts. He may say: *"Tisaraṇena saddhim pañca-sīlaṃ dhammaṃ sādhukaṃ surakkhitaṃ katvā appamādena sampādethā'ti"*. The last two words are also the last ones uttered by the Buddha at Kusinara before his Final Nibbana. The passage means: "Three Refuges together with the Five precepts having been taken for one's welfare, guard (them) well (and) with mindfulness make an effort!".

In Thailand it is usual to chant:
"Imāni pañca-sikkhāpadāni
Sīlena sugatiṃ yanti
Sīlena bhogasampadā,

Sīlena nibbutiṁ yanti
Tasmā sīlam visodhaye."

This means:
"These (are) the Five Rules of Training
Keeping these Precepts one may go to the happy bourns
Keeping these Precepts become wealthy, (worldly/Dhamma)
Keeping these Precepts gain the Cool (Nibbana),
That is why these Precepts should be kept in purity."

The Pali in this common Buddhist ceremony is sometimes explained line by line in the vernacular Thai in Thailand, except when westerners receive these Refuges and Precepts when they are followed by English explanations.

This concludes the Going for Refuges and Precepts and a person who has done so then again makes the triple prostration having placed all his faith in these Refuges. They are truly safe Refuges for one is really taking Refuge in the Enlightened One, the Way to Enlightenment, and in Teachers who are 'Ones-Who-Know'. No other Refuges are necessary, for in these one has the highest already. In order to practise so that these Refuges are realized in Enlightenment as three inward Gems, the Five Precepts are taken. They are the first step to Enlightenment.

The Buddha has said:
"But going for refuge to Buddha,
To Dhamma and the Sangha too,
One sees with perfect wisdom,
The tetrad of the Noble Truths."

Dhammapada 190.

A SUMMARY OF BUDDHIST SCRIPTURES

What did the Buddha say? Various collections exist of works call Sutta (Pali) or Sutra (Sanskrit), or of which open with the words "Thus have I heard". These are counted by the various Buddhist traditions as the words of the Buddha. However, Buddhists generally are not dogmatic about this and regards these various 'scriptures' (many of them were originally chanted, not written down) as indications of how to practise and not literally words spoken by the Buddha.

Three great collections in three different languages now exist: in Pali, Chinese, and Tibetan. Scriptures in Sanskrit and other Indian languages were mostly lost with the destruction of Buddhism in India. The collection mostly used in Thailand is the Pali Tipitaka (literary, Three Baskets) called by westerners, 'The Pali Canon', although in Chinese temples the Chinese Tripitaka is found.

Most of the books in the Pali Canon have been translated only once, very few have two or three translations, while only one book (the Dhammapada) has been translated some thirty times into English. The summary noted below is of the Canon in Pali—near to the language spoken by thr Buddha—the works of which even if not complete are very extensive.

The Pali Canon was the result of slow collection and enrichment of the Buddha's words through the first Three or Four Councils. This Canon was then transmitted by 'memorizers'—bhikkhus who learnt portions of the discourses, etc., by heart from their Teachers, and in turn transmitted the memorized text to their bhikkhu-pupils. This verbal transmission continued for about 400 years. There is evidence that some material has been lost, exactly how much we cannot say.

Due to the disturbed conditions of those times, the senior bhikkhus in Sri Lanka decided to commit the whole Canon to writing. They assembled for this purpose and wrote down the Buddha-word using the metal stylus to inscribe 'ola'or palm leaves. In tropical climates these will last 400 years or so. Since that time the Canon was copied using the same materials until printed editions began to appear at the end of the nineteenth century. The first complete printed edition was published by order of His late Majesty, King Rama the Fifth (Chulalongkorn), using the Thai script.

In the West, the Pali Text Society (P.T.S.) was founded by Dr. T. W. Rhys Davids in 1881, for the publication of the entire Canon in Roman script. This is now complete and most of it has been translated into English and published by the same society.

The Pali Canon is composed of the following sections and subsections. The list below includes the titles of the published translations of the P.T.S. followed by their literal meaning. Beginners who wish to dip into the riches of these works are advised to read first the translations marked with an asterisk.

PALI TIPITAKA

I. VINAYA-PITAKA: The Book of the Discipline (Basket of Discipline). Six books in complete translation from P.T.S.

    1.   **Bhikkhu-vibhanga**—the analysis of discipline for bhikkhus.

    2.   **Bhikkhuni-vibhanga**—the analysis of discipline for bhikkhunis.

    3.   **Mahavagga**—the great collection of miscellaneous disciplines.

---

1. For more detail see Russell Webb, 'An Analysis of the Pali Canon', Wheel No. 217–200, B.P.S., Kandy.

4.   **Cullavagga**—the lesser collection of miscellaneous disciplines.

5.   (**Parivara**—a summary composed in Sri Lanka).

[**Bhikkhu-patimokkha** (an extract from 1. above)—the 227 training-rules for a bhikkhu published by Mahamakut Press, Bangkok.]

II. SUTTA-PITAKA: No P.T.S. Title (Basket of Discourses).

Twenty- nine books in translation so far. P.T.S. titles first:

*1.   **Digha-nikaya**—Dialogues of the Buddha (The Long Collection) 3 books containing 34 long discourses. New translation: Long Discourses of the Buddha, Wisdom Publications, Somerville, 1987.

2.   **Majjhima-nikaya**—Middle Length Sayings (The Middle Collection) 3 books containing 152 discourses of medium length. New translation: The Middle Length Discourses of the Buddha, Wisdom Publications, Somerville, 1995.

3.   **Samyutta-nikaya**—Kindred Sayings (The Related Collection) 5 books containing (traditionally) 7762 discourses arranged into 56 groups by subject. New translation soon to be published.

4.   **Anguttara-nikaya**—Gradual Sayings (The Numerical Collection) 5 books containing (traditionally) 9557 discourses arranged in numerical books from one to eleven.

5.   **Khuddaka-nikaya**—Minor Anthologies (Minor Collection) composed of fifteen separate works:

*i.   **Khuddakapatha**—Minor Readings and Illustrator—its Commentary. A brief handbook for novice monks/nuns.

*ii.   **Dhammapada**—Path of Truth (many translations) 26 chapters containing 423 inspiring verses. For its Commentary, see note at end.

*iii. **Udana**—Verses of Uplift (Inspired Utterances of the Buddha). New translation, B.P.S., Kandy, 1997.

*iv. Itivuttaka—As it was said (Sayings), a collection of short discourses. New translation: The Buddha's Sayings, B.P.S.

*v. Sutta-nipata—Group of Discourses/The Rhinoceros Horn. Another new translation is The Sutta-nipata, Ven. Saddhatissa, Curzon Press, London, 1985.

vi. Vimanavatthu—Stories of the Mansions—accounts of the heavens.

vii. Petavatthu—Stories of the Departed—accounts of the ghosts.

*viii.Theragatha—Psalms of the Brethren/The Elders' Verses I (two translations, both P.T.S.)—inspired verse uttered by Enlightened bhikkhus.

*ix. Therigatha—Psalms of the Sisters/The Elders' Verses II—the same for bhikkhunis.

*x. Jataka—Jataka Stories—'550' (actually 547!) past lives of the Buddha in three volumes (only verses are canonical, stories are commentary).

xi. Niddesa—(Analytic Explanation)—no English translation of this ancient commentary on (v) above.

xii. Patisambhidamagga—The Path of Analysis—analysis of different dhammas and ways of practice.

xiii. Apadana—no English translation of these past lives of disciples.

xiv. Buddhavamsa—The Chronicle of the Buddhas—accounts of the Buddhas of the past.

xv. Cariya-pitaka—Basket of Conduct—a short collection of Jataka stories arranged to illustrate the Perfections.

III. ABHIDHAMMA-PITAKA: No P.T.S. title. (The Basket of Further Teachings) Six books in translation so far.

1. Dhammasangani—Buddhist Psychological Ethics.
2. Vibhanga—The Book of Analysis.
3. Dhatukatha—The Discourse on Elements.
4. Puggalapannatti—A Designation of Human Types.

5.   **Kathavatthu**—Points of Controversy—added at the Third council.

6.   **Yamaka**—no English translation.

7.   **Patthana**—Conditional Relations.

Among the Commentaries on the above, few of which have been rendered into English, the Dhammapada Commentary, a collection of stories translated under the title of "Buddhist Legends",* is strongly recommended (P.T.S., 3 volumes). Also good reading is the account of the questions asked by the Indo-Greek King Menander of the great Bhikkhu Nagasena, under the title of "Milinda's Questions" (P.T.S., 2 volumes). An older translation is also available: "Questions of King Milinda", Motilal Banarsidass, New Delhi.

MAHAYANA SUTTA

There is no society which issues these and most are published commercially. A selection of these Sutra would include:

The Large Sutra on Perfect Wisdom, E. Conze, New Delhi, Motilal Banarsidass, 1990.

The Perfection of Wisdom in 8000 in Lines and its Verse Summery, E. Conze, Bolinas, Four Seasons Foundation, 1973.

The Short Prajnaparamita Texts, E. Conze, London, Luzac and Co. Ltd., 1973.

Buddhist Wisdom Books (Diamond Sutra and Heart Sutra), E. Conze, London, George Allen & Unwin Ltd, 1958.

The Teaching of Vimalakitri, Etienne Lamotte trans. Sara Boin, London, P.T.S., 1976.

The Sutra of the Golden Light, R. E. Emmerick, London, P.T.S., 1990.

The Threefold Lotus Sutra, Bunno Kato et al, New York, Weatherhill/Kosei, 1982.

The Lions Roar of Queen Srimala, A&H. Wayman, New York, Columbia University Press, 1974.

The Lankavatara Sutra, D. T. Suzuki, Boulder, Prajna Press, 1978.

Buddhist Yoga (Sandhinirmocana Sutra), T. Cleary, Boston, Shambhala, 1995.

A Treasury of Mahayana Sutras, C. C. Chang, Pennsylvania State University Press, 1983.

INDEX